PEACE WITH

THE PSALMS

PEACE WITH

THE PSALMS

40 READINGS TO RELAX YOUR MIND

AND CALM YOUR HEART

DEVOTIONS FROM

ABIDE CHRISTIAN MEDITATION

ZONDERVAN BOOKS

ZONDERVAN BOOKS

Peace with the Psalms
Copyright © 2021 by Carpenter's Code, Inc.

Requests for information should be addressed to:
Zondervan, *3900 Sparks Dr. SE, Grand Rapids, Michigan 49546*

Zondervan titles may be purchased in bulk for educational, business, fundraising, or sales promotional use. For information, please email SpecialMarkets@Zondervan.com.

ISBN 978-0-310-36336-1 (audio)

Library of Congress Cataloging-in-Publication Data

Names: Abide Christian Meditation (San Mateo, California), author.
Title: Peace with the Psalms : 40 readings to relax your mind and calm your heart / Abide Christian Meditation.
Description: Grand Rapids : Zondervan, 2021. | Includes bibliographical references. | Summary: "Peace and comfort are attainable, even when your heart is at its most restless. For readers seeking peace and comfort in even the most trying circumstances of life, Peace with the Psalms by Abide Christian Meditation offers forty readings of the best of the Psalms, encouraging a regular, relevant, and transformative connection with Jesus"—Provided by publisher.
Identifiers: LCCN 2021010001 (print) | LCCN 2021010002 (ebook) | ISBN 9780310363347 (hardcover) | ISBN 9780310363354 (ebook)
Subjects: LCSH: Bible. Psalms—Meditations. | Bible. Psalms—Prayers and devotions.
Classification: LCC BS1430.54 .A25 2021 (print) | LCC BS1430.54 (ebook) | DDC 242/.5—dc23
LC record available at https://lccn.loc.gov/2021010001
LC ebook record available at https://lccn.loc.gov/2021010002

All Scripture quotations, unless otherwise indicated, are taken from The Holy Bible, New International Version®, NIV®. Copyright © 1973, 1978, 1984, 2011 by Biblica, Inc.® Used by permission of Zondervan. All rights reserved worldwide. www.Zondervan.com. The "NIV" and "New International Version" are trademarks registered in the United States Patent and Trademark Office by Biblica, Inc.®

Scripture quotations marked NLT are taken from the Holy Bible, New Living Translation. © 1996, 2004, 2015 by Tyndale House Foundation. Used by permission of Tyndale House Publishers, Inc., Carol Stream, Illinois 60188. All rights reserved.

Any internet addresses (websites, blogs, etc.) and telephone numbers in this book are offered as a resource. They are not intended in any way to be or imply an endorsement by Zondervan, nor does Zondervan vouch for the content of these sites and numbers for the life of this book.

Cover design: Studio Gearbox
Cover image: © Zamurovic Brothers / Shutterstock
Interior design: Denise Froehlich
Edited by: Stephanie Reeves and JoHannah Reardon
Written by: Drew Dickens, Stephanie Reeves, JoHannah Reardon, Russ Jones, Jennifer Waddle, Michael Foust, Amy Peterson, Cortney Whiting, Jennifer Stoltzfus, Maggie Bruehl, Chris Maxwell

Printed in the United States of America

21 22 23 24 25 /LSC/ 10 9 8 7 6 5 4 3 2 1

CONTENTS

DEDICATION

This book is dedicated

To the talented team of writers at Abide in the past and present whose work appears in this book. To Drew Dickens, whose fingerprints are all over the scripts from the beginning. To Amy Peterson, one of our first writers, whose talent in bringing God's Word to people is deeply appreciated. To Stephanie Reeves, who lends not only her gift for writing but her keen eye for editing to every meditation. To Jennifer Waddle, whose gift of encouragement can be felt throughout the pages. To Russ Jones, who along with serving as the executive producer of Abide, also brings his heart for God's people to these meditations. To Michael Foust, who has a gift for description and for exhortation to be true to the Word of God. To Cortney Whiting, an early writer for Abide, whose work has touched many lives. To Jenn Stoltzfus, who jumped in with both feet in her enthusiastic, no-holds-barred way. To Maggie Bruehl, who while fighting her own cancer battle, found the heart to want to encourage others in their relationship with God. To Chris Maxwell, whose words encourage and inspire wherever they are found. Thank you all for pouring your hearts into these profoundly comforting words from God's truth!

———————

To my wife, Nadia. Thank you for your unwavering support.

———————

To my mother, Sarah. Thank you for trusting me to follow God's plan.

———————

To JoHannah Reardon, coeditor of and contributor to this book, who passed away on February 4, 2021, after an eighteen-month battle with cancer. JoHannah's editor's eye, heart for God, and love for his people are evident throughout the pages of *Peace with the Psalms*. We are grateful.

———————

NEIL AHLSTEN
CEO of Carpenter's Code

INTRODUCTION

"This app has brought me so much peace." We hear this over and over again from our Abide listeners, and it's always a humbling statement. In a world where anxiety, depression, and turmoil are becoming such a struggle in the lives of so many people, I've wanted Abide to be a place where above all, people find the *peace* of God.

I left Google to start Abide with CTO Eric Tse because I felt the need to slow down and take time to know and hear from God more diligently, more regularly. What became evident very quickly after we started our company was that helping people with the anxiety they were facing should become a high priority of ours. According to the Anxiety and Depression Association of America, anxiety disorders are the most common mental illness in the US, affecting 40 million adults in the United States age eighteen and older, or 18.1 percent of the population, every year.[1] And that number reflects merely the people who have sought help. Many more who suffer anxiety will never seek professional counseling or even share what they are facing with someone. Research shows that this surge in anxiety is only continuing to grow as myriad forces converge and combine to make modern life uniquely challenging—and dangerous. Since the long-term effects of stress and anxiety on the body are considerable, we all must learn to develop and adopt strategies that can help relieve this avoidable pandemic.

The great news is that our Abide app users have already discovered and benefited from a remedy generations of Christians around the world have long known about: the Psalms.

In creating this book of our most sought-after content, our goal with these daily meditations and story reflections from the Psalms was to provide an experience of the *peace of Christ* different from any you may have had before. The Psalms are full of wise admonitions about learning to put our trust in God, which is proven to help us to relax in the assurance that he is in control when we definitely are not.

If you feel anxious about the state of the world, your relationships, your finances, or something else, biblical meditation has a unique and incisive power to relieve that anxiety by focusing your thoughts on God's presence and faithful promises. In fact, physical or mental health conditions are also no match for praying the Psalms, as countless readers and app users have found. In forty days, these short daily entries can help you experience the comforting knowledge that Jesus is always with you in your suffering and is providing his Spirit to guide you in praying for healing. If you are under spiritual attack, the Psalms remind and reassure of scriptural truth and of the all-powerful hand of God to protect you against all enemy attacks, provide deliverance, and restore the peace that surpasses all understanding. If you are dealing with recurring sin in your life or separation from God, the Psalms help you experience the grace, salvation, and regeneration of Jesus' life in you that brings joy and lasting contentment. If you lie awake at night, as many do, with too much running through your head, the Psalms can help you slow your mind back down to remember how God is calling you in quiet moments to live the healthier, reconnected life you long for.

In many of the meditations in this book, you will be asked to visualize places and imagine yourself in ways you may never have before. You'll be guided through exercises intended to instill a fuller awareness and sense of God's presence, which brings the peace that only he provides. Let the prayers at the end of each chapter become your own words, and try not to hurry through. Then, when you've finished the day's reading, linger a few moments and just be with God as your mind explores the new thoughts and feelings you've found.

My hope and prayer is that you not only enjoy this unique book, but that you might find it helps you grow your trust in the One who loves you beyond all comprehension or comparison, and who will never, ever let you go.

May you always abide in Christ.
NEIL AHLSTEN
CEO of Carpenter's Code

WHY BIBLICAL MEDITATION?

"Mindfulness" is in. Slowing down, taking time just to breathe. Being aware of your surroundings and your body. Experts tout not just the mental health benefits but the physical benefits as well.

According to an October 15, 2020, article on the website PositivePsychology.com, the benefits of mindfulness include a decrease in stress, an enhanced ability to deal with illness, and a decrease in depressive symptoms.[2]

Who wouldn't want all that, right?

So what makes *biblical* meditation different? Instead of just focusing on your feelings and senses, letting your body control where your thoughts go, how does focusing on God and his Word change us in profound ways?

Psalm 1:1–3 says,

> Blessed is the one
>> who does not walk in step with the wicked
> or stand in the way that sinners take
> or sit in the company of mockers,
> but whose delight is in the law of the LORD,
>> and who meditates on his law day and night.
> That person is like a tree planted by streams of water,
>> which yields its fruit in season
> and whose leaf does not wither—
>> whatever they do prospers.

Meditation has gotten a bad rap with some Christians who see danger in the term. The rise in Eastern mysticism and the practice of "emptying your mind" or practicing "new age" religion has scared them off the word. But contrary to some thinking, meditation did not originate with Eastern mysticism and the birth of Siddhārtha Gautama, who became known as the Buddha (c. 563 BC to c. 483 BC). Genesis, where the word *meditate* is first used in Scripture ("[Isaac] went out to the field one evening to meditate, and as he looked up, he saw camels approaching," Genesis 24:63), is thought by Bible scholars to have been written between 1450 and 1410 BC. Most agree that the evidence indicates that the practice of meditation predates the Buddha by some eight hundred years, rooting it squarely in the Judeo-Christian tradition.

Biblical meditation, therefore, is a practice from the Bible that has been refined for thousands of years. It connects and empowers our minds and hearts in Jesus. It helps us live with the peace and purpose of Christ. According to Thomas A. Tarrants III, president emeritus of the C.S. Lewis Institute, "Meditation is a devotional practice that we engage in with God's help to know Him better, love Him more, experience closer communion with Him, and live for His glory."[3]

Our focus as Christians should be *what* we choose to meditate on. We hear from our Abide listeners all the time about the peace they have found as they have deepened their relationship with God through the biblical meditations on our app. People who have been taking sleep aids for years are now able to sleep deeply through the night as they go to bed listening to God's Word through our sleep stories. And the word we hear probably more often than any other? *Peace.*

Is there a person among us who doesn't need more peace in their life? Unless you live in a cave and never have any contact with the outside world, you have been touched by turmoil. King David of ancient Israel knew turmoil. He spent a lot of time actually in caves, hiding from his enemies. And during those times, he penned many of the psalms in the Bible. He would cry out to God and lament his situation. But he always came back to God.

Psalm 5, for instance, starts out, "Listen to my words, LORD, consider my lament. Hear my cry for help, my King and my God, for to you I pray." But it ends with "Surely, LORD, you bless the righteous; you surround them with your favor as with a shield."

And Psalm 10 starts out, "Why, LORD, do you stand far

off? Why do you hide yourself in times of trouble?" But it ends with "You, LORD, hear the desire of the afflicted; you encourage them, and you listen to their cry, defending the fatherless and the oppressed, so that mere earthly mortals will never again strike terror."

Our goal in this book is to help you appropriate the peace of God by leading you in meditating on the truths found throughout the book of Psalms. Don't rush off after you read each day's meditation. Spend some time in prayer, connecting with your heavenly Father. Consider memorizing the verse that begins each meditation.

And "may God himself, the God of peace, sanctify you through and through. May your whole spirit, soul and body be kept blameless at the coming of our Lord Jesus Christ" (1 Thessalonians 5:23).

THE LORD IS MY SHEPHERD: PSALM 23

The Lord is my shepherd, I lack
nothing.
He makes me lie down in green
pastures,
he leads me beside quiet waters,
he refreshes my soul.

—PSALM 23:1-3

 Imagine it. Lying down in a beautiful lush green pasture beside a quiet, soothing stream. Not a care in the world. Only feeling refreshed, restored, protected, guided, consoled, and loved. Yes, there are shadows. There is darkness. But never so oppressing that you fear it. Because God is with you. He has been, he is, and he will be for all eternity.

Whether or not your life feels peaceful doesn't change the fact that your Father in heaven is the Good Shepherd and is present to love and care for you.

Imagine God's eyes, how he looks at you, the intense care and love. The look that says he knows everything about you yet loves you anyway. It's impossible for him to love you any more than he does right now.

Imagine the pastures he gives you. Feel the cool grass as you look up at the blue sky. The warmth on your face. Soak up everything you imagine around you. Can you hear the birds twittering happily? A gentle breeze stirs your hair. Smell the sweet scent of the grass and the nearby wildflowers. You are in a safe haven. A wide-open space well guarded by your loving Shepherd.

Hear water bubbling nearby. Gentle. Soothing. Refreshing. Hear it. Smell it. Dangle your feet and toes in it. It is there to soothe you. You dip your cupped hand in and pull out a handful of the cool water. You lean your head down to drink. Ahhh. Feel the life that it gives you. Drink deeply of the Living Water that is Jesus within your soul.

He leads you along the right paths for his name's sake. Not wandering, but guided down a path. His light shines on that path. His Word is a lamp for your feet to keep you from stumbling. His rod protects you. His staff guides you.

Even though you walk through the sunless valley, you will fear no evil, for you are with him. No storms surprise God. No thunder bothers him. No shadows catch him unaware. He is with you. You are his forever.

He prepares a table before you in the presence of your enemies. Sit at the table he has prepared. See all the gifts he has laid out before you. He has anointed and refreshed your head with oil. Your cup overflows. His blessings don't just fill you; they overflow.

Surely goodness and mercy and unfailing love shall follow you all the days of your life, and you shall dwell forever, throughout all of eternity, in the house and presence of the Lord.

Our gracious, heavenly Father, our Good Shepherd, thank you for leading me to this green pasture, for making me to lie down and rest. May I feel your presence all around me; help me to revel in the goodness you have brought me. May I hear your voice of comfort and feel your hands of care on me. When I am afraid, may I trust in you, knowing you care for me so very much. Take all worry away, Lord, as you walk with me through the valleys. Remind me moment by moment of your care and provision for me. Help me to relax, Lord, knowing that you will stay by my side. You will never leave me nor forsake me. As numerous as the stars are in the sky or as the grains of sand are on all the beaches in the world, so vast is your love for me. Let your love envelop me like a blanket, keeping me safe and warm. Let your clear waters restore my soul. Amen.

A TIME TO DANCE:
PSALM 33

Sing joyfully to the Lord, you
  righteous;
    it is fitting for the upright to
    praise him.
Praise the Lord with the harp;
    make music to him on the ten-
    stringed lyre.
Sing to him a new song;
    play skillfully, and shout for joy.

—PSALM 33:1-3

 A spirit of joy is a delight to the soul! But it's not always easy to come by. Sometimes our emotions get in the way. What is hindering you from experiencing joy in the Lord?

I invite you to take your eyes off your circumstances and instead to focus on God himself so that you can receive the joy that he has for you—joy *in him*, which is so different from the world's.

God is glorious and deserving of our praise! When we turn our gaze on his wonderful face, our hearts are freed to sing of his mighty works, to bask in his loving-kindness and vast love for us. With everything we are and with all that we do, we can praise him. All of creation tells of his glory. Waves crash, thunder rolls!

For his mighty deeds, praise him. According to his excellent greatness, praise him. With every breath that you have, praise him. In a loud, glad, exalting voice, praise the God of the heavens and the earth. The psalmist calls on everything that has breath to praise the Lord!

As you turn your heart to a spirit of praise, lift your eyes to the heavens. See God's glory all around you in his creation. The trees of the field clap their hands in praise to him. The birds of the air are fed and clothed by him. Let your heart soar as you see all that he has done around you and in you.

Music is often something you can use to quiet your heart and bring steadiness to your soul. Those peaceful times are renewing and invigorating. And then comes the loud crashing of the cymbals in joyous celebration of the goodness and greatness of God—the joy and the dancing that bursts forth from the very depths of your soul as you remember all that God is and all that he has done for you!

We are told in Zephaniah 3:17 that God will exult over us with loud singing and that he will rejoice over us with gladness. Imagine listening to his words of love for you and reflecting them back to him as you realize in a deeper and deeper way how much he loves you.

In Psalm 33:3 the psalmist urges you to write a new song, one filled with joy and praise to the God who *does* wonders and *is* wonderful. The great God of the universe is your audience. He is eager for your every word. Let his joy suffuse your heart, mind, and soul so that it spills out of your lips as you stand before him and praise him in the midst of all creation! Praise the Lord!

Oh Lord, Psalm 8:1 says "how majestic is your name in all the earth!" I might not be a world-class musician. I might not have the voice of an angel. But all that I am is yours, and with every breath I take, I want to praise you. You are good; you are sovereign; you are mighty. No power on earth can best you. Thank you for your love and care for me. You are worthy of praise! Open my eyes to see your wonders. Remind my heart of how worthy you are of my praise every moment of every day. Yes, I have struggles in this life, but you never change even though my circumstances do! I'm so very grateful for all that you are and all that you have done. May I never grow weary of praising you. Amen.

SAVOR HIS FAVOR:
PSALM 5

Listen to my words, LORD,
    consider my lament.
Hear my cry for help,
    my King and my God,
    for to you I pray.

In the morning, LORD, you hear my voice;
    in the morning I lay my requests
        before you
    and wait expectantly.

—PSALM 5:1-3

 Do you have a lament for God today? Perhaps something that is weighing on your heart? God invites us to lay our requests before him, and then to wait patiently in the presence of the Lord as you savor the gift of God's favor.

And just in case you are wondering, God's favor is the undeserved grace that he chooses to give because he loves and delights in us.

So settle your mind on the gift of God's love and delight over you. Receive his undeserved grace, and know that he loves you with an everlasting love.

Allow the words from Psalm 5 to stream over you and through you, as living water for your soul.

Now let me tell you a story. A young man walked along the beach at night. He was agitated and praying and seeking God's will for his life. As he walked, he looked for a sign of God's favor, begging God to show up.

As he stood at the ocean's edge, letting the cool water lap over his feet, he looked up at the moonlit sky, thanking God for his magnificent creation. He marveled at the fact that God knew each star by name—stars as numerous as the sand on the seashore!

Then something in the distance caught his eye. It was a unique star formation—one he had never seen before. The stars were in the unmistakable shape of a cross! And as he gazed upon that cross in the night sky, he immediately sensed the Lord say, "My dear child, I have given you everything through my Son, Jesus."

The young man's life was changed that night. God heard the cry of his heart. All of his prayers were poured out to the

Father on the moonlit beach that night. And by God's grace, he was reminded of what he had already been given.

The gift of God's favor is unmerited and undeserved. Yet, through his Son, it is given freely to all who will receive it.

Receive the gift of God's favor through Jesus today.

> Listen to my words, LORD,
>> consider my lament.
> Hear my cry for help,
>> my King and my God,
>> for to you I pray.

Rest in the presence of your King and your God.

Better is one day in the house of the Lord than a thousand elsewhere. Feel the holiness of his presence as you envision being in the house of the Lord, kneeling before his throne.

God's righteousness was given to us through the sacrifice of his Son. In Jesus Christ alone, we are shown the way. All the crooked places are made straight. Every confusing idea is clarified in him. And we know that he will make his way clear before our eyes.

The gift of God's favor is truly a gift.

Unmerited and undeserved, his love delights our souls. And through his limitless grace and mercy, he gives us the gift of his favor.

Feel the blessing of God on your life. Through the gift of his favor, and with his presence as a shield, rest peacefully today.

Holy God, keeper of our souls, please keep me in the fold of your arms, day and night. Right where I am, cradle me in the gift of your favor. Be my shield and protector. Help me set my mind on heavenly things— things that are promised for me. Continue to show yourself in the wonders of creation and remind me that through your Son I have received the gift of your favor, forever and ever. Amen.

WAITING IS DIFFICULT:
PSALM 13

How long, Lord? Will you forget me
    forever?
  How long will you hide your face
     from me?
How long must I wrestle with my
    thoughts
  and day after day have sorrow
     in my heart?
  How long will my enemy triumph
    over me?

—PSALM 13:1-2

 David wrote this psalm in a time of great stress. Imagine that you are with King David and his men, hiding in a cave, surrounded by your enemies. You don't know whether God will vanquish them and save you or not. You wait, not knowing what the end result will be.

Now, shift from what David experienced to what you have to wait for. A child? The results of medical tests? Waiting is not easy. It can feel like God has forgotten about you. But are your feelings based on fact? Has God forgotten you? The answer to that question, of course, is no, God has not forgotten, but his timetable rarely aligns with ours.

When you find yourself in a season of hard waiting, what can you do to keep trusting God?

How do we prosper in our relationship with God when he seems to take so long in answering our prayers? We know from experience that God's answers are usually one of three things: yes, no, or wait. Most often it's "wait," and we need to be patient to see what he does over time.

King David was overwhelmed by his circumstances. His enemies were constantly attacking him, and in his pain, he didn't see how God was ever going to show up again. He was in anguish. But if we read to the end of Psalm 13, we find these words:

> But I trust in your unfailing love;
>> my heart rejoices in your salvation.
> I will sing the Lord's praise,
>> for he has been good to me.

David didn't know what the outcome of his predicament

would be, but he knew God's character. He is good. All the time. And that ultimately was enough for him.

We, too, can put our hope in the Lord through our seasons of waiting. We can trust that he is good and always acts for our good. And in that knowledge our waiting becomes our strength:

> But those who hope in the LORD
>> will renew their strength.
> They will soar on wings like eagles;
>> they will run and not grow weary,
> they will walk and not be faint. (Isaiah 40:31)

So in your waiting, draw nearer to God instead of pushing him away. Pushing might be what you feel like doing, but God's promises hold true whether he answers in your timing or not.

Amazingly enough, your soul could be strengthened in your waiting. Both Isaiah and David testify to this fact. Hymn writer Thomas Chisholm wrote, "Strength for today and bright hope for tomorrow."⁴ Take those words to heart and repeat them aloud. It will be a healing balm to your soul.

In your hardest waiting, imagine going through your worst-case scenario. *What if . . . I never get to be married? What if . . . I never have children? What if . . . I lose my child or my spouse or my parents?* End each scenario with the words, "Yet God."

Is it the possibility that what you're waiting for will not come to pass that causes your fear and pain? If you face those fears and are still able to say along with Job, "may the name of the LORD be praised" (Job 1:21), the waiting will be more bearable.

Consider memorizing verses 5 and 6 of Psalm 13 to return praise to the Lord and let him know that you trust him in your waiting. Practice repeating it as you wait for the smaller things in life, like a stoplight or your turn in line.

Dear Lord, your Word says that creation groans, waiting for all things to be made new, so it is no wonder that I also groan in my waiting. Help me to trust you with what I cannot yet see. Help me to be patient in my waiting, to seek you, to stay by your side. In my waiting, grow my faith. Help me know that you have not forgotten me. Thank you that though I don't know what my future holds, I know you. I know that you are good; I know that you love me. I know that you are sovereign over all things. In my seasons of waiting on you, help me to remember these things and to draw close to you. I don't want to push you away, because then I would have nothing. I love you. Amen.

NEAR TO THE BROKENHEARTED: PSALM 34

The righteous cry out, and the LORD
   hears them;
  he delivers them from all their
    troubles.
The LORD is close to the
   brokenhearted
  and saves those who are crushed
    in spirit.

The righteous person may have
   many troubles,
  but the LORD delivers him from them all.

—PSALM 34:17–19

Many years ago, there was a popular song written by Scott Krippayne called "What Breaks Your Heart." It included the lyrics, "Sometimes You weep with us in the things that we go through."[5] Suggesting God's tenderness toward us when we are brokenhearted, the song reminds me of Psalm 34.

One of the reasons God is able to understand our brokenness so intimately is because he experienced it himself. When Jesus walked the earth, he went through extreme brokenness, not only on the cross, but in many of his daily interactions with people. Ultimately, he was despised and rejected. He longed for people to accept him as their Savior and Messiah, yet they mocked him and crucified him.

When we face difficult trials on this earth, it's easy to get so discouraged that we start to believe God has distanced himself from us. Our faith may begin to waiver as we wonder if God will really deliver us out of the hardship. When life seems to be a series of one hardship after another, it's understandable that we would get disheartened and think that God doesn't hear us. However, God does hear our cries for help.

None of us wants to know what it feels like to be "crushed in spirit," as Psalm 34 says. That is perhaps one of the worst experiences we could go through. The Hebrew meaning of "crushed" in this passage indicates a contrite or devastated spirit. In the garden of Gethsemane, Jesus sweat drops of blood because of the agony of spirit he was in. Yet he prayed, "Not my will, but yours be done" (Luke 22:42).

The apostle James acknowledged that in this life we *will* have trials of many kinds (James 1:2). But God promises us in Psalm 34 that he is near us when we are brokenhearted, he hears us when we cry, and he delivers us out of every trouble.

Will you allow yourself to believe that right now? Let your mind rest in the comfort and compassion of God. He is with you!

As you think of the struggles of your day, remember to go to your first line of defense—Jesus himself. And rest in his peace today.

Holy God, please forgive me for doubting that you can deliver me from every trial. When the hardship lasts too long, I start to feel like you are far away. Please help me to know you are near. I commit all of my brokenness to you today. I'm waiting excitedly to see how you will deliver me from all my afflictions. Thank you for being near me when my heart is broken and I am crushed in spirit. Lord, it is comforting to know that you understand fully the things I am going through. I ask that you help me to know your comfort and compassion, that I might sense your presence and draw strength from you. I praise you for defending me and upholding me with your righteous right hand. In the name of Jesus I pray. Amen.

UNBURDENED: PSALM 4

In peace I will lie down and sleep,
for you alone, Lord,
make me dwell in safety.

—PSALM 4:8

 Imagine for a moment that you are hiking along a beautiful mountain trail. When you started, the pack on your back didn't feel very heavy at all. You were excited for your journey and started out quickly.

But now, after walking for a while, you feel the weight of that pack. You can't even remember what all you packed. You're pretty sure you thought everything was important at the time, but it's beginning to weigh you down. It's taking away the enjoyment and wonder of the beautiful scenery around you. That's not what you want from this time of refreshment. You want to be free from your burdens.

While you are not carrying a physical pack, you may be

carrying an emotional and mental one. Take a moment now to let go of those worries and concerns that are weighing you down. If you are anxious about something, rather than being ashamed, offer that anxiety to God. Remember that Jesus said you could cast your cares on him (1 Peter 5:7). Picture your worries like rocks in a backpack. Take them out, one by one, and hand them to Jesus. If those worries show up in your backpack again, that's okay; just give them to Jesus again. He is your ever-present help in times of trouble (Psalm 46:1). He does not grow weary, and he desires to give you his peace.

Having surrendered your worries and fears to God, feel the lightness in your spirit. You don't have to carry those things anymore. You're free of them. Feel the weight gone from your shoulders. Feel the muscles of your neck and back loosen and relax, free of the burden they were carrying.

Sense the presence of God with you, shielding you from all harm. You are in an utterly safe place when you are trusting God. Allow that sense of complete safety to guide you into deeper rest. You don't have to remain vigilant. You don't have to worry about anything. God is here. God is good. God is in control. You can surrender to God, knowing that he is love. Not a single muscle in your body needs to be tense right now. God will fight for you all day long. God will deliver you.

God is your protector, defender, and deliverer. You have nothing to fear, for God is with you. He hears and answers your prayers. He stays with you through the day and all through the night, never leaving or forsaking you. New mercies will be waiting for you every morning when you wake.

Feel God's presence like a blanket over you, offering comfort, warmth, and protection. Sink deeply into that comfort. Wrap it around your relaxed limbs. Imagine yourself taking refuge in God and singing for joy. Imagine what that looks like: where you are, who is with you, and what God says as he looks at you. God delights over you with singing.

Oh Lord, you keep me safe in peace, rest, and restoration. You comfort me. You desire to give me all good things. You hear me when I call to you, and you give me gladness and joy. Now, dear Father, fill me with peace and a sense of safety. Allow me to feel your presence, to know that you are near, and that you are ever watchful. God of all comfort, comfort me. You have taken all my burdens upon yourself. Give me a sense of the freedom you've granted. Draw me deeper into your rest, your peace, and your love. When I lie down to sleep tonight, may I sleep in peace, for you alone, Oh Lord, make me dwell in safety. And may I wake in the morning refreshed with your song of joy in my heart. In the name of Jesus I pray. Amen.

SWEETER THAN HONEY: PSALM 19

The fear of the Lord is pure,
    enduring forever.
The decrees of the Lord are firm,
    and all of them are righteous.

They are more precious than gold,
    than much pure gold;
they are sweeter than honey,
    than honey from the
        honeycomb.

—PSALM 19:9–10

 Everyone who has working eyes has seen the sky. It spreads over our heads both day and night. You don't hear it speak. It doesn't have words. Yet it proclaims the glory of God in its very existence. From the soft pastel colors of sunrise to the brilliant display of sunset, God's majesty speaks.

The Word of God, on the other hand, often speaks loudly and clearly in our hearts and minds. We hear it preached, we listen to it read, and Psalm 19 reminds us that every word of it is true and can be trusted.

Imagine you're sitting inside your house, where it's warm and comfortable, in your favorite armchair. You have worked all day, and it's time to take off your shoes and settle in to spend some time alone.

On the sturdy table beside you sits your Bible, its soft leather cover worn by years of use. Next to it is a pile of work you brought home that you could get some extra money for if you completed it tonight. The thought is tempting.

And then you think about that carton of ice cream just sitting there in your freezer. Its sweetness entices you. The thought of that icy goodness causes your taste buds to burst in anticipation.

And then you glance again at your Bible. You remember how the words it contains have fed your soul time and time again.

Psalm 27:13: I remain confident of this: I will see the goodness of the Lord in the land of the living.

Hebrews 13:5: Keep your lives free from the love of money and be content with what you have, because God has said, "Never will I leave you; never will I forsake you."

John 10:10: "The thief comes only to steal and kill and

destroy; I have come that they may have life, and have it to the full."

Your heart quickens as the Spirit of God brings these words to your mind.

Psalm 42:1: As the deer pants for streams of water, so my soul pants for you, my God.

Romans 5:8: But God demonstrates his own love for us in this: While we were still sinners, Christ died for us.

On and on God's life-giving words fill you up. You forget about the extra work beside you. You forget about the ice cream in the freezer. In your hand is all you need. God's promises are true. His words are life-giving.

Imagine that as you go about your day with the Lord, you open your heart to his gaze. You want every part of you to be seen, cleansed, and available to him. You want every thought and every action to be pleasing to him.

You say with the psalmist, "May these words of my mouth and this meditation of my heart be pleasing in your sight, LORD, my Rock and my Redeemer" (Psalm 19:14).

Heavenly Father, may your watchful eye be ever upon me in love and grace. As I go about my day, may I experience the awesomeness of your glory whenever I look at the sky. May I see your wonders in the sun and the clouds. In the evening, may the sunset remind me of your love and great compassion, and may the stars speak silently to me of your majesty and your intimacy, for you know them each by name. As I sleep, give me peaceful, satisfying dreams, and if I awake in the night, may your holy, trustworthy words be ever in my thoughts. God, you are my rock and my redeemer, my firm foundation. Thank you for reminding me that you are mighty yet gentle, everywhere at once, yet close by my side. In the name of Jesus I pray. Amen.

MY WHOLE HEART: PSALM 9

I will give thanks to you, Lord, with
all my heart;
I will tell of all your wonderful
deeds.
I will be glad and rejoice in you;
I will sing the praises of your
name, O Most High.

—PSALM 9:1-2

 With words of praise from King David—a song of his heart—we are encouraged to offer our whole hearts in worship and honor of the living God. Let those words, "in worship and honor of the living God," sink deeply into your mind as you take this time of reflection and offer your whole heart to the Lord.

David begins this beautiful psalm by saying,

> I will give thanks to you, LORD, with all my heart;
>> I will tell of all your wonderful deeds.
> I will be glad and rejoice in you;
>> I will sing the praises of your name, O Most High.

And he continues,

> My enemies turn back;
>> they stumble and perish before you.
> For you have upheld my right and my cause,
>> sitting enthroned as the righteous judge. . . .
> The LORD is a refuge for the oppressed,
>> a stronghold in times of trouble.
> Those who know your name trust in you,
>> for you, LORD, have never forsaken those who
>> seek you.

How can we make these words a reality for our lives?

You know, children have a way of saying exactly what's on their minds—honest and uninhibited. They feel free to dance in the living room, sing at the top of their lungs, and tell fantastical stories that their innocent minds imagine. It's that childlike wonder that keeps them from bottling things up and holding back. Often they put their whole hearts into what they're doing, as they play, imagine, dream, and worship God freely.

Allow that childlike wonder and freedom to flow through your own heart and mind.

The late gospel singer Aretha Franklin was just a girl when she recorded an album called *Songs of Faith*. As an adult, she recalled singing in her father's church and developing a love for music and worship that followed her throughout her life. She told of a time when she and her older sister were driving at night and a particular song came over the radio and they stopped the car, got out, and actually danced on the highway!

It's that kind of "sweet abandon" that the Lord desires of our praise. Allow that imagery to settle over you for a few moments.

Breathe in the goodness of God. He loves you. Do you know that? His love reaches far beyond the heavens. There is no limit to his love. You are never beyond his reach.

> Remain in the Lord's presence.
> Linger in his love.
> Abide with him.

The Lord welcomes you like a little child. Jesus told his disciples, "Let the little children come to me, and do not hinder them, for the kingdom of heaven belongs to such as these" (Matthew 19:14).

Like a precious child, rest unhindered in the arms of Jesus.

Trust in the One who loves you, who keeps his word, who showers you with grace and mercy. I wrote this poem just for you.

I will praise you with my whole heart;
Nothing will get in the way.
No sickness, toil, or worry
Will prevent my worship today.

I will praise you with my whole heart
Amid the dark of night,
For you alone deserve my praise,
My hope, my strength, my light.

I will praise you with my whole heart
In wakefulness and sleep.
In childlike faith I trust you
My heart forever to keep.

Dear friend, seek the Lord, put your trust in him, and rest deeply in David's comforting words. Feel God's presence in the room. Feel his shield around you, his protection. Allow yourself to rest in safety, provision, and peace.

Heavenly Father, keeper of our hearts, please abide with me and help me to trust in your care. Flow through my mind with words of truth and steadfast promises. Turn all of my troubled thoughts into songs of praise. With my whole heart, mind, soul, and strength, may I rest in you. Softly and tenderly, as Jesus calls my name, I pray that I will heed your call and be restored to a childlike faith and trust in you. For it is in the precious name of Jesus I pray these things. Amen and amen.

NO NEED TO FEAR: PSALM 27

The Lord is my light and my
salvation—
whom shall I fear?
The Lord is the stronghold of my life—
of whom shall I be afraid?

—PSALM 27:1

 David had been on the run for quite a while. He had been loyal to King Saul, but Saul had betrayed him and sought to kill him. By this, David knew that Saul was not just going against him but against God. They both knew that God had chosen David to succeed Saul, yet Saul refused to accept that.

To combat his fears, David liked to write songs. Imagine him pulling a slab of damp clay in front of him and then picking up the stiff reed he used as his writing tool. As was often the case, the words would begin to flow freely.

> The LORD is my light and my salvation—
> whom shall I fear?
> The LORD is the stronghold of my life—
> of whom shall I be afraid?

What comfort these words brought David. As he sat in a dark cave, he reflected on how the Lord was his light. The Lord was the One who would ultimately rescue him. David knew better than to trust in his own puny power.

And as David spent his life on the run, he found great joy in remembering that the Lord was his stronghold, more secure than the most powerful fortress.

When God is your light, salvation, and stronghold, your own fears greatly diminish. Picture the Lord standing at your side with his mighty heavenly army coming against your fear. Let that image give you confidence.

More than anything, David wanted to dwell in the house of the Lord, which meant that he wanted to be in God's presence. David knew that God was with him, even in this dark cave, but he longed to worship him publicly before all of Israel.

Imagine David's dejection as he thought about how he was barred from the places he'd come to love. But as he looked out over the fields of Israel, even on the run, he was able to see God's handiwork. He knew that the Lord was even more beautiful than his creation. He found great comfort in that. The Lord's beauty is overwhelming and awe inspiring.

The Lord kept him safe, sheltered him, and set him upon the high rock. Even if he wasn't on the literal high ground, he was certainly on the spiritual high ground. Through Christ, God has set you on the high ground spiritually, and because of that miraculous work in you, you can make music in your heart to him.

David had cried out to God in anguish, his emotions getting the best of him. But now he lowered his arms and put one foot down firmly to help his body and heart follow his mind.

David didn't know how long it would take for God to vindicate him and put him on the throne. He didn't know how long it would take for Saul to quit pursuing him. But he did know one thing: because God was his protector, he had no reason to fear.

Our heavenly Father, I have nothing to fear, for you are with me. You are my light and salvation. Nothing can stand against me. Sometimes it seems like I have to wait and wait and wait for your help to come, yet I know you hold me in your strong arms. And I am so grateful. Thank you for calming all my fears and never leaving my side. Remind me of that throughout the day and when I ready myself to sleep tonight, and bring it to mind if I wake in the night. In the name of Jesus Christ I pray. Amen.

JOY COMES IN THE MORNING: PSALM 30

Weeping may stay for the night,
but rejoicing comes in the morning.

—PSALM 30:5

Do you have sorrow in your heart over some hard things in your life? Maybe you have spent many a night soaking your pillow with your tears over a lost family member, a tragedy around you, a burden you just can't bear anymore.

If the nights are long, the sorrow is unrelenting, and you are wondering if it's ever going to end, Psalm 30:5 makes it clear: it is going to end. Sorrow will not have the last word in your life. Sickness and disease will not have the last word in your life. Whether you're in a dark, hard time right now or storms are on the horizon, know this: it is temporary.

King David wrote in Psalm 30:5 that "weeping may stay for the night, but rejoicing comes in the morning." Yes, joy comes in the morning, but when does *morning* come? How long will it be until the sun shines again?

Imagine yourself in the scene with King David as he is praising God for hearing his prayers, for bringing him out of the pit, for healing him. David's life has been given back to him, and he wants you to know about it and celebrate with him. He has just come out of a very difficult season, a time of trouble and deep distress, and now he wants you and all your friends to join him in prayers and songs of thanksgiving to the God who answered his prayers. He invites you to pray with him. He calls out to everyone who can hear, "Sing the praises of the LORD, you his faithful people; praise his holy name."

David looks right at you. He wants you to join him in thanking God and singing God's praises, because God listened to his cries for help and saved him. And he will do the same for you.

Dear child of God, your mourning, your sorrow lasts only until morning; when the night is gone, the gloom shall vanish. Jesus has conquered sin and death. He has risen in victory over them, and he will have the last word. He has been called the bright Morning Star (Revelation 22:16). Where Jesus is, there is no more sorrow. He is the Light of the World. He brings light into the dark places. He redeems your soul from the pit. Know that mourning will turn into dancing. Joy comes with the morning.

Heavenly Father, thank you for the reassurance that the struggles and sorrows of this world are ultimately temporary. Thank you that one day hurt will be no more, that one day you will wipe away every tear from my eyes. You will turn my mourning into everlasting dancing and gladness. Please calm my racing thoughts. Carry the burdens that sometimes make each waking hour a dread rather than a joy. Carry me to a place of divine serenity and oneness with you. Bring calming rest to my soul, full of peaceful thoughts and visions of a renewed life. In the name of Jesus I pray, amen.

I LIE DOWN AND SLEEP: PSALM 3

I lie down and sleep;
   I wake again, because the Lord
     sustains me.
I will not fear though tens of thousands
   assail me on every side.

—PSALM 3:5-6

King David wrote Psalm 3 after he and his court had fled Jerusalem in the middle of the night. Tragically, his jealous son Absalom had been leading a rebellion to dethrone David. Eventually those rebels even tried to kill him. Those traveling with David were exhausted, discouraged, and hungry. It would have been easy for David to doubt God's goodness.

But in the midst of this, King David's faith in God

remained strong. And he saw God provide food and supplies for his hungry people through friends on two different occasions, prompting him to center his thoughts on Jehovah.

And then he wrote,

> Lord, how many are my foes!
>> How many rise up against me!
> Many are saying of me,
>> "God will not deliver him."

> But you, Lord, are a shield around me,
>> my glory, the One who lifts my head high.
> I call out to the Lord,
>> and he answers me from his holy mountain.

> I lie down and sleep;
>> I wake again, because the Lord sustains me.
> I will not fear though tens of thousands
>> assail me on every side.

> Arise, Lord!
>> Deliver me, my God!
> Strike all my enemies on the jaw;
>> break the teeth of the wicked.

> From the Lord comes deliverance.
>> May your blessing be on your people.

King David often wrote music, but this song had special meaning. It encouraged the people in their trials. It gave hope in the midst of great adversity. King David's army eventually defeated Absalom, and the king and his royal court returned to Jerusalem. As David's psalm said, he called out to the Lord, and the Lord answered him. He lay down to sleep, and God sustained him.

God remained faithful and good. He always does.

God—the creator of the universe—is also watching over you. He's protecting you. He's a shield around you. He's the lifter of your head. He gives you hope. When you call out to the Lord, he answers—just as he answered David.

When you lie down and sleep, he sustains you.

You have no reason to fear because . . . "from the LORD comes deliverance."

You are a child of God as surely as David was. Just as a loving parent cares for a child, God is caring for you right now.

Rest in his loving arms. Abide in his mighty presence. Accept God's gift of peace.

Dear Father, thank you that I am your precious child. I praise you for being my shield and protector. Thank you for being the lifter of my head. Now, Father, I ask that you grant me peace. Your Word says, "I lie down and sleep; I wake again, because the LORD sustains me." I ask that you will help me to find rest in you. When I lie down to sleep tonight, may I wake up refreshed, ready to serve you another day. I pray in Christ's name. Amen.

WHITE KNUCKLES:
PSALM 119

How can a young person stay on
the path of purity?
By living according to your word.

—PSALM 119:9

 I love roller coasters. The anticipation, buckling in, my heart pounding, the clacking as I go up the first hill, the way time stops at the top, and then holding on through the endless loops, turns, and rollovers. It's funny, though. I know I'm buckled in securely, but I hold on tight, so tight that my knuckles turn white. Why? Because in my heart I don't believe the seat belt will hold me, even though it's been tested by engineers with PhDs. I need to white-knuckle it just to make sure.

I sometimes do the same when it comes to trust in the

Lord. Even though the creator of the universe says he has my life in his hands, I white-knuckle it just to make sure. Maybe if I squeeze and hold on a little tighter, I can manage this next wave of temptation myself. How has that practice worked out for you?

The author of Psalm 119 asked a pertinent question: How can a young person live a clean life? And then he answered: by living according to God's Word. Notice what's missing in that verse. It doesn't say to try a little harder. It doesn't say we can stay pure by holding on tighter and hoping for the best. Consider ways that you hold on a little tighter out of your own strength rather than letting go and trusting God's strength. How much of your fight to live the Christian life is by your strength instead of God's?

Being self-aware—aware of when you are taking on the fight alone—is key.

Joshua was Moses's second-in-command. He was a great leader who walked with God's people into the promised land. But the people were afraid. And rightly so. They had heard stories of giants and soldiers in the land. But God told Joshua to be strong and courageous (Joshua 1:6)!

What does that mean for you? Read the Scriptures. Day and night think about what they say. Ask God for strength and courage to obey them. *Then trust him.* If you do that, you will not need to white-knuckle it, and you'll have nothing to fear.

So slip onto the roller coaster. Trust the seat belt as the Word of God. Trust the bar that locks in around you as God's presence. Trust the engineers who designed the ride as the promises of God. Yes, it's still scary as the ride starts, but how does it feel as the coaster comes back in after the ride? Ready to go again? Each ride makes you stronger.

Dear heavenly Father, white-knuckling it can be exhausting. And when it comes to my relationship with you, white knuckles are useless. Help me to let go. Help me to surrender to you on this ride. When I face temptations, trials, and tragedies, help me to live a clean life by living according to your Word. Please help me to put, and keep, my trust in you with all my heart, and help me not to depend on myself and white knuckles for peace and understanding, remembering that you abide in me and I abide in you. I offer and pray this in the name of Jesus, your Son, our Savior, and my Lord. Amen.

DESIGNED TO BE JOY-FILLED: PSALM 16

You make known to me the path of
life;
you will fill me with joy in your
presence,
with eternal pleasures at your
right hand.

—PSALM 16:11

 Have you ever experienced joy, even during a time in your life when things were not going well? Joy can be yours despite your circumstances, because joy isn't based on circumstances.

Why? Because Jesus lives outside of time and space. And he is perfectly good, perfectly loving, and full of grace. In

Jesus' presence, you can experience the joy that fills heaven. Imagine that!

Does that kind of joy seem beyond your reach right now? If so, don't despair. Sometimes in the worst of circumstances, God gives the deepest joy: A woman has been diagnosed with brain cancer, yet her face radiates peace and her voice gives testimony to God's faithfulness. Parents give birth to a gravely disabled child. Yet through their great sorrow and tears, evidence of the joy they have in their relationship with God can be seen. They cling to him with all they have because he is their anchor. Their words testify to God's greatness.

There is no earthly explanation for their behavior. Their joy is simply from being in God's presence.

Of course, everyone wants to feel happy and joyful. But if you keep waiting to "feel" happy, you'll miss out on the fullness of joy that God wants to give. If you've ever wandered from Jesus, you have experienced the lack of joy that brings. When we choose to go it alone, our hearts long for more. But in Jesus' presence, there is joy.

God created you because it delighted him to do so. Joy is in God's character. And he wants his joy to be in you. You were designed to be full of joy. There are various definitions of *joy* today. One definition says that joy is a "feeling of great happiness." Another says that joy is "the emotion evoked by well-being, success, or good fortune." Probably the definition closest to the word translated "joy" in the Bible is "the emotion of great delight or happiness caused by something exceptionally good or satisfying."[6] Jesus is the One who is exceptionally good and satisfying.

God is always active in your life. He makes his path of life known to you. He encourages you. He gives you strength. And he offers you his joy. Jesus has given you eternal life, and nothing can change that. God is with you always, and nothing can change that. Whatever situations you may face, you always have the option of joy—a joy based on eternal realities, not temporary things.

We may experience many temporary joys in this life, but God says that complete joy is found only in his presence.

Dear Father God, you know my circumstances. Thank you that you understand every hardship, pain, and trial. I want to have your joy in every situation and season. Please draw me nearer to you. Open my eyes to see more of who you are. Thank you for the gift of your Son, Jesus. I believe that knowing him is the greatest joy there is. And as difficult as this life can be at times, I know it is temporary. Please help me learn to seek your presence in every circumstance. Draw me near to you and teach me more about your joy. In the name of Jesus, amen.

MY HELP COMES FROM GOD: PSALM 121

I lift up my eyes to the mountains—
where does my help come from?
My help comes from the Lord,
the Maker of heaven and earth.

—PSALM 121:1-2

Imagine that you are in a peaceful valley. It's lush and green with glorious rolling hills that rise and fall into the distance. Wildflowers dot the landscape with vibrant color. Yellow daffodils. White jasmine with sweet-smelling petals. You walk slowly through the valley in perfect peace, breathing the fresh spring air. Up above you see a clear blue sky with wispy clouds floating overhead. Stillness and peace surround you. You are fully content and completely relaxed in the valley.

As you walk through the beautiful green valley, the gentle, rolling hills rising up around you, you know where your help comes from. He is walking beside you in glowing robes, the risen Lord. He is peace. You are immersed in a sense of stillness and security.

As you look around that valley at the magnificent landscape, you *know*, just by the beauty of creation, that God is your creator, your provider, your help.

Feel his presence now. He is with you in the valley. God the Father calls out to you from the hills. Your heart rejoices at his voice. You call out to him, and before a word is even on your tongue, he knows it. He is already sending the help you need at just the right time and in just the right way. How can you know this? Romans 8:26 says, "The Spirit helps us in our weakness. We do not know what we ought to pray for, but the Spirit himself intercedes for us through wordless groans." He knows what you need. He is always there for you.

Be amazed by the faithfulness of God, the One who does not slumber or sleep. He never grows weary. He is a constant presence in your life. You have nothing to fear.

Even in the night watches, when the way seems dark and unfamiliar, your foot does not stumble. His Spirit leads you.

The safety you feel in the crook of the Lord's loving arms is the most secure feeling in the world. All the cares of life have faded into the night. You are able to breathe deeply and know that you are completely safe. No evil can touch you. For the Lord is keeping you from everything that is harmful or contrary to his love for you. Your very life is held fast in the palm of his hand. You've never felt so protected. It's as if walls of love have been placed around you so that nothing can reach you. You are surrounded by God's perfect peace.

As you go through the valley and find pasture, your life is locked in and secured in the fold of the Great Shepherd. He watches over your coming and going. Nothing escapes his sovereignty. He keeps watch over you from this time forth, now and forevermore.

Gracious God, thank you for your protection over me. Help me always to remember that my help comes from you alone. Hold me in the fold of your tender, loving arms. I pray for a sense of peace and security as I remember that you love and care for me. Give me visions and dreams of your hope. Refresh me each day. Be my help in times of need, and allow me to sleep deeply whenever I lay down my head. In the name of the Father, the Son, and the Holy Spirit, amen.

PRACTICING GRATITUDE: PSALM 92

It is good to praise the LORD
and make music to your name,
O Most High,
proclaiming your love in the
morning
and your faithfulness at night.

—PSALM 92:1-2

 Does it sometimes feel like more is going wrong in your life than is going right?

When times are tough, it isn't always easy to give thanks to God. But sometimes when life is hardest, you can be renewed by praising God.

That's what Psalm 92 tells us. Whether the past week has been filled with joy or with hardship, or a combination of both, your soul can flourish by pausing and giving thanks, acknowledging that even in difficulty God has been present and God has provided. His love has been steadfast and faithful, always with you.

Psalm 92 is traditionally sung on the Sabbath—the day of rest. It is the only psalm in the Hebrew text that is designated as a Sabbath psalm. I wonder what it is about praise that brings rest for our souls?

It is good to give thanks to the Lord and to sing praises to God. Perhaps you've seen this goodness in your own life as a result of practicing gratitude even in difficult times. The psalmist said that he sings joyfully when he sees the works of God's hands, and that he delights in God's deep wisdom.

Maybe the idea that God's thoughts are very deep and beyond our comprehension feels more frightening than inspiring to you. You may feel frustrated by your own inability to understand God's ways. But the psalmist takes comfort in God's wise, incomprehensible ways.

Imagine what it might look like to spend a whole day practicing gratitude for the goodness of God: When you wake up, before you check your phone or turn on the shower, you say good morning to God. You say, "God, thank you for your kindness." As you walk through your day, you practice giving thanks in all things—thanking God for your coffee or tea, thanking God for the traffic or the lack of traffic, thanking God for the sunshine or the rain.

As your day comes to a close, rather than falling asleep at your desk or with the television or your mobile device on, you end the day rejoicing in the specific ways God has been faithful to you. Give thanks for the ways he protected you and for how he has guided you in the rightness of his wisdom. As you look back, you see that he was with you in each moment. Could today be a day like the one you've just imagined, a day bookended by prayer and praise, a day filled with the awareness that God is with you and filled with thanksgiving for his provision moment by moment?

I invite you to practice gratitude. As you do, perhaps you will find that your soul begins to sing to God.

Most High God, I declare with the psalmist that you are worthy of praise. You are my rock and my redeemer! I can rest because you are in control. Your love is constant and faithful. Your provision never ends. Your mercy is perfect and your grace is complete. You gave me your only Son to save my soul. You sent your Spirit to live in me. Wow! I am in awe of you. And I praise your name! Fill my heart with thankfulness and joy. In the name of your precious Son, Jesus, I pray. Amen.

THE GIFT OF SLEEP:
PSALM 127

In vain you rise early
and stay up late,
toiling for food to eat—
for he grants sleep to those
he loves.

—PSALM 127:2

 Perhaps you've never thought of sleep as a gift from God. But it is. Sleep is a beautiful gift of peace and rest that comes from the Father's hand. Let's unwrap the gift of sleep today.

Imagine your loving creator handing you a beautifully wrapped package. He encourages you to untie the ribbon and let it fall away. He guides you to remove the wrapping and set it aside. He waits patiently as you open the box to discover a beautiful gift—the gift of sleep.

Sleep is a gift, for it allows us to process, restore, and strengthen our bodies and minds. As we drift through the sleep cycles, our mind is able to sort out the day's events. We are able to organize information, file it away, and remember what is most important. Each cell in our bodies benefits from sleep. Sleep rejuvenates us, repairs our tissues, and restores us after a long day of hard work.

Oh, what a beautiful gift from our heavenly Father! Since he created us, he knows just what our bodies need, so he created sleep. And not only do our physical bodies need sleep, but our spirits need God's true rest.

Now, be assured that rising early, at the start of a new day, ready to work with willing hands, is a good thing. Starting the day with an anxious heart, however, isn't beneficial at all.

Instead of rising early with burdens on your heart, consider starting your morning with a quiet meditation. Let God's Word be the first words you hear each day. For his mercies are new every morning.

Then, as you move through your day, no matter what comes, you can recall the sweet words of wisdom you heard that morning. You can carry his Word with you as a guide, a comfort, and a peaceful meditation.

At the end of the day, resist the temptation to keep working and toiling into the night. Read the wise words of Solomon who, in verse 2 of Psalm 127 said, "In vain you rise early and stay up late, toiling for food to eat—for he grants sleep to those he loves."

Often, when sleep eludes us, it's because we are holding on to the cares of this life. We struggle to let go of them because we struggle to trust God. We forget that God is sovereign over us, and he has given us sleep as a gift.

Dear one, the Lord watches over you when you wake and when you lie down. Imagine him keeping watch over you.

Thank you, good Father, for the gift of sleep. Thank you for knowing just what I need at the end of a long day. Help me to release every worry and concern to you. Please cover me with your peace and protection so that I can fully relax and find true rest in your presence. Help me to surrender my life to you and receive the gift of true rest. I pray I find comfort and peace in your presence. Please help me to let go of anything that is on my mind or in my heart. Thank you for loving me. Thank you for watching over me. Thank you for the gift of sleep. Amen.

LIFT UP YOUR VOICE! PSALM 40

He put a new song in my mouth,
   a hymn of praise to our God.
Many will see and fear the LORD
   and put their trust in him.

—PSALM 40:3

 When you're suffering and waiting for deliverance, what do you do?

When God rescued King David and gave him a new song to sing, many people witnessed the greatness of God's saving love. The song God gave David led many other people to put their trust in God.

God has delivered you from the power of sin and death. He has rescued you from the kingdom of darkness and brought you into the kingdom of his Son. Let your heart respond with joy and thanksgiving for all that God has done for you. Ask God to reveal his power in your life and to use what he does to draw many other people to worship him.

Consider the fears, worries, and stresses that have been weighing you down. God is calling you to turn these over to him, to trust him with them.

Imagine that you're out for a walk on a pleasant day, but suddenly the ground gives way beneath you, and you slide into a pit. You didn't see this coming! You didn't choose it. But you find yourself in the dark, covered with mud. You've fallen so far, you can barely see the light above you.

When you cry out for help, your voice seems to echo in the emptiness of the pit. But God hears you. Before you know it, you're being lifted out, hosed off, and set on solid ground—ground that won't give way beneath you.

On this new, steady ground, you find a song welling up within you, and as you walk along the path, you begin to sing.

Lots of people saw your rescue. Even more are listening to your song. They begin to come up to you one by one or in small groups to ask you questions about who saved you and what just happened.

What would your song sound like? I imagine it would be a song of great praise to the one who rescued you, the one who pulled you out of that muddy pit. You might not feel like you can write psalms of praise like the ancient psalmists could, but with whatever fills your heart today, you can praise God. Lift up your voice! He is worthy of your praise.

God, your wonders are too many to count. Don't hold back your tender mercies from me. Let your unfailing love and faithfulness always protect me. Put a new song in my heart, and I will sing of your love forever. You are the One who delivers. By your mighty power, your unfailing love, and the life, death, and resurrection of your Son, Jesus, you rescued me from sin and brought me into your kingdom. I will sing your praises forever. Thank you, God. In the name of Jesus I pray. Amen.

STANDING ON LEVEL GROUND: PSALM 143

Teach me to do your will,
    for you are my God;
may your good Spirit
    lead me on level ground.

—PSALM 143:10

When you pray in faith during a hardship, does that mean that you believe that God *will* deliver you from this trial or that he *is able to* deliver you? Sometimes all we want is for the ground under our feet to be level. I'm guessing Job felt that way. His world certainly was shaken when he lost everything all at once.

When you continue to face trials, it is difficult to pray with heartfelt, humble, believing, and obedient prayer. But these prayers are where God's good Spirit can lead us to solid, level ground in the midst of an earthshaking quake.

Did you catch the three parts in Psalm 143:10? The first and the third—"teach me to do your will" and "lead me on level ground"—are perfect bookends to the middle. Why? "Because you are my God" is always the *why*. Doing his will is not for our purpose but his. This principle can be reflected in your times of prayer. Reflect deeply and practice focusing on him more and you less (or, more honestly, you *none*) in your times of prayer.

So the bookends are "teach me" and "lead me." Teach me to follow God and lead me to level ground. Note that the verse actually says, "may your good Spirit lead me on level ground." Picture that when you spend time in prayer. Imagine his hand in yours. Feel level, smooth ground beneath your feet.

Psalm 25:4–5 is a beautiful and similar passage:

> Show me your ways, LORD,
>> teach me your paths.
> Guide me in your truth and teach me,
>> for you are God my Savior,
>> and my hope is in you all day long.

The apostle Paul wrote a letter to the growing church in a city called Colossae in what is present-day Turkey. He wrote the letter to help the Colossians understand more deeply who Christ is. He wrote,

For this reason, since the day we heard about you, we have not stopped praying for you. We continually ask God to fill you with the knowledge of his will through all the wisdom and understanding that the Spirit gives, so that you may live a life worthy of the Lord and please him in every way: bearing fruit in every good work, growing in the knowledge of God, being strengthened with all power according to his glorious might so that you may have great endurance and patience, and giving joyful thanks to the Father, who has qualified you to share in the inheritance of his holy people in the kingdom of light. (Colossians 1:9–12)

Knowledge of who God is and a willingness to let his Spirit guide you are key to abiding on level ground. Find strength for that journey in God's Word, where he can teach you more and more about himself.

Dear prayer-answering God, please give me the strength today to stop often and ask for your help and your guidance. Please give me your words, your heart, your desire for prayer that is heartfelt, humble, believing, and obedient. Teach me to do your will so that I may please you, for you are my God; and may your good Spirit lead me on level ground. It is in the name of Jesus I pray. Amen.

CREATE IN ME A CLEAN HEART: PSALM 51

Create in me a pure heart, O God,
and renew a steadfast spirit
within me.

—PSALM 51:10

 Most of us long to make ourselves clean and full of good qualities so that we can find favor with God. But this verse in Psalm 51 flies in the face of that. David asked God to create in him a pure heart. In other words, he knew it was beyond his own ability, and that he needed God to do it for him.

King David understood the gravity of needing to be cleansed by God in order to have a pure heart. After his adultery with Bathsheba, David was confronted by Nathan the prophet, and in response to feeling convicted of his sin, he cried out to the Lord for a renewed heart and spirit.

This was the same David who, years earlier, was commended for being a man after God's own heart. And he was! However, just like all of us, David needed a reminder that only God can make the heart clean and the spirit holy. Our attempts at holiness can go only so far.

When we look back to the beginning, the moment God created Adam and Eve and breathed life into them, we see his original design for humankind, which was for us to have clean hearts and right spirits within us. He longed for us to walk in perfect unity with him.

However, it wasn't long before Adam and Eve strayed from perfect unity with God. Satan duped Eve by turning her focus from God to the desires of the flesh. Once she gave in to her fleshly desires, her heart became stained with sin.

David's psalm of cleansing came after he had committed the sins of murder and adultery. Even in his deepest regret, he knew that God was a just God, willing to forgive.

And in the New Testament, 1 John 1:9 tells us that when we confess our sins, God is faithful and just to forgive us and cleanse us from all unrighteousness.

Sometimes doubt or self-condemnation prevents us from receiving God's cleansing power. We mistakenly believe that we are "too far gone" to be made new. But that simply is not true. God longs to make you new today! All he asks is that you have a willing heart to receive.

Psalm 51 has some wonderful insights into how David

prayed for renewal. In verse 12 he said, "Restore to me the joy of your salvation and grant me a willing spirit, to sustain me." Sometimes we forget this truth and allow our daily struggles to cloud our vision and diminish the joy we have in Christ Jesus.

To have a "willing spirit," we need to fix our mind on the things the Holy Spirit desires: Love, joy, peace, forbearance, kindness, goodness, faithfulness, gentleness, and self-control. All of those characteristics are listed in Galatians 5:22–23 as fruit the Holy Spirit will develop in our lives when we trust in God.

Toward the end of Psalm 51, David admitted that only with a humble spirit could he present himself before the Lord. He said, "My sacrifice, O God, is a broken spirit; a broken and contrite heart you, God, will not despise."

Are you broken before the Lord? Do you need to be cleansed?

Sandra Felton, author of *The Messies Manual*, gives practical tips for deep cleaning and organizing your house. She advises starting at the front door and working your way around the room from right to left and top to bottom, providing a methodical plan for getting every room in your house in order.[7] Likewise, we can formulate a plan for decluttering our minds and preparing our hearts to receive God's complete cleansing. Starting with humility, we can make ourselves submissive to God through prayer. Then we can move on to worship, letting joy and praise filter out the "cobwebs" of our souls. Lastly, we can read the Bible and allow the washing of the Word to cleanse us by the working of the Holy Spirit.

Whether you are getting ready to start your day or about to go to sleep, or somewhere in between, know that God is here to forgive you and embrace you so that you can experience his peace.

Gracious God, I know that only by your Spirit am I made new. I need your cleansing touch. Thank you for your conviction, as I remember that only you can renew my heart, mind, and spirit. There is nothing I can do in my own self to be pure or holy. Only by your cleansing power am I made righteous before you. Thank you for giving me a clean heart and a right spirit. I want nothing more than to be a person after your own heart. I surrender the ways in which I've tried to make myself clean enough, for it is only by your grace that I stand. In the name of Jesus I pray, amen.

ARE YOU WEARY?
PSALM 145

The Lord is near to all who call on
    him,
    to all who call on him in truth.
He fulfills the desires of those who
    fear him;
    he hears their cry and saves
    them.

—PSALM 145:18–19

 Did you know that if your heart beats 75 times a minute on average, that means your heart beats 108,000 times a day, and your blood travels twelve thousand miles every twenty-four hours?[8] It is no wonder that you sometimes (often?) feel tired! Not only do our bodies accomplish amazing feats, but we also must contend with life's daily pressures and temptations.

Life is a battlefield. Maybe at times you long to be the hamster on the wheel, never seeming to run out of energy. But sometimes your energy supply runs its course hours before the sun goes down. On these days, it is easy to feel defeated and alone. Yet Jesus tells us to come to him when we are weary and heavy burdened, and he will give us rest (Matthew 11:28). The Lord does not want you merely to survive; his desire is for you to thrive.

Your heavenly Father loves you and cares for you. As an ever-present God, he always hears your prayers. When you feel that you have no strength, the Lord promises to provide. He does not leave his children empty. In him is salvation, deliverance, and life. As his child, your responsibility is to trust in him. When you feel weary, with faith like a child, cry out to your Father, who hears you and longs to comfort you in your distress.

There is a difference between being tired and being weary. When we're tired, physical rest can revive us. But when we're weary, only the peace of God will suffice to make us strong again. We can get caught up in doing all kinds of terrific things, but if we're going above and beyond what God wants us to do, we can get worn out, weary. Overexertion, not getting enough rest, or even a lack of movement can cause our bodies to feel tired. Weariness is more soul deep.

Do you ever find yourself going out on a limb to do

something for someone else, a "good" thing, only to find that the limb won't support your weight? You crash to the ground, right? But when you are doing what God has called you to do, you have the strength of an eagle. Your spirit is renewed. You can soar. Even if you fall because of your own actions, he is always there to pick you up and give you rest. Your only job is to abide in Christ and do what he tells you to do.

We worship a God who is able to do immeasurably more than all we ask or can imagine. That is how big our God is. Rest in the knowledge that he is a good and loving Father who desires the best for his children. Whether you find yourself in a moment of energy or a moment of weakness, remember that you serve a God who hears you when you call. Rest well in that glorious knowledge.

Dear Lord, as I take a moment to think of how you desire for me to come to you, even in my weakness, I am in awe of how much you love me. Thank you for wanting me to share everything about me, even what makes my heart ache. Help me to use even my tiredness to honor you. I stand on the promise that you are the Lord who is near to me in the moments when I am strong and when I am weak. Thank you for always meeting me when I cry out to you. Thank you for answering me when I call. Even when I feel like I have no strength to journey on, help me trust in you to carry me. In the name of Jesus I pray. Amen.

GOD WILL SUSTAIN YOU: PSALM 55

Cast your cares on the Lord
  and he will sustain you;
he will never let
  the righteous be shaken.

—PSALM 55:22

 If you live where earthquakes happen, you know what it's like to be shaken suddenly, without warning. Sometimes the quake can last a few seconds, and other times it can last a few minutes. It's always unsettling.

When something happens that seems like more than you can handle, it can feel like an earthquake in your life. Surely that is how it felt to David each time King Saul tried to kill him and when his son Absalom rebelled against him.

David wrote Psalm 55 after one of those "earthquakes," and yet in verse 22 he reminded us, "Cast your cares on the LORD and he will sustain you; he will never let the righteous be shaken." David knew that God wouldn't let him be moved away from the purpose he had given him.

When you encounter an earthquake in your life, what do you do? Do you toss and turn at night, your thoughts whirling? Or do you cast your cares on him? Do you stand on the firm foundation of God's promise to sustain you?

Trusting in God's promise to sustain you is easier said than done. Perhaps you've tried to cast your worries on Jesus, then felt overwhelmed by the weight of them again. But no matter how bad your circumstances are, God promises to hold you up. He will support you and nourish you. He will work out his own good purposes for your life. His power is greater than your weakness. His grace is greater than your need. And his purposes are greater than what you can see right now.

Ephesians 6:10–18 shows how you can use the Word of God to stand firm no matter what circumstances threaten to undo you. It speaks of putting on the whole armor of God, that you may be able to stand against the schemes of the devil: the belt of truth, the breastplate of righteousness, feet fitted with the readiness that comes from the gospel of peace, the shield of faith, the helmet of salvation, and the sword of the Spirit, which is the Word of God.

You have all the tools you need to stand firm, even when earthquakes threaten to shake up your world, because the

Spirit of God lives within you. He has promised to sustain you. The word *sustain* can mean to hold up, to support, or to nourish. Throughout David's life, God faithfully protected him, delivered him, and kept him close to his heart. Trust that he will do the same for you.

> *Father, sometimes the weight of my circumstances threatens to crush me. I feel my feet slipping, and I cannot stand. But I know you are still there. Help me to see you. Help me to remember your promise never to leave me nor forsake me. Set my feet on the solid ground of your Word, that I might not be moved. Thank you for sustaining me and upholding me. I trust in you. Thank you for this encouragement from your Word. Lord, you know how weak I feel and how difficult my circumstances are. I choose to give my burdens to you, and I ask you to sustain me one moment at a time. Please pour your supernatural strength into me so that you can accomplish greater things than I can ask or imagine. Let me see how you're sustaining me. Strengthen my heart to trust that you are working out your good plans for me even through my suffering. Amen.*

SING SONGS OF
TRUTH: PSALM 59

But I will sing of your strength,
    in the morning I will sing of your love;
for you are my fortress,
    my refuge in times of trouble.

—PSALM 59:16

They call them earworms—songs that get stuck in your head long after they're over. You can't stop singing them, hearing them in your mind, no matter what you try. If it's a commercial jingle or annoying chorus, it can be maddening.

How much better to let the truths of God become earworms so that you can't stop hearing and singing the greatness of your God. Instead of being annoying, they can be a balm and a comfort to your soul. They can lift you up with joy.

What truths about God do you need to sing over and over again?

Think of the truths embedded in the Trinity: God is strong and steadfast, an ever-present help in times of trouble. The Holy Spirit is our guide and comforter, giving us power over the enemy, indwelling us, filling us. And Jesus is the embodiment of God's presence. God among us. Our Savior, redeemer, and friend.

Wrap yourself in this truth: because of Jesus' death and resurrection, you have been liberated.

What does that mean? You are completely free. Your chains have been removed. Guilt has fled. Shame no longer identifies you. Instead, you are identified as a child of the King of Kings. You are no longer known as a sinner. How refreshing that knowledge is!

What if you made up your own song? What if you sang the words of praise from Psalm 59:16: "strength," "love," "fortress," "refuge"? Let your words become a chorus to God, a symphony, a song of praise.

The book of Psalms is a songbook, so consider adapting some of its songs and making them your own. For example:

Psalm 21:13: Be exalted in your strength, LORD; we will sing and praise your might.

Psalm 143:8: Let the morning bring me word of your unfailing love, for I have put my trust in you. Show me the way I should go, for to you I entrust my life.

Psalm 101:1: I will sing of your love and justice; to you, LORD, I will sing praise.

Psalm 5:3: In the morning, Lord, you hear my voice; in the morning I lay my requests before you and wait expectantly.

Psalm 88:13: But I cry to you for help, Lord; in the morning my prayer comes before you.

Or you might download some of the great hymns of our faith: "Amazing Grace," "How Great Thou Art," "Holy, Holy, Holy," or "It Is Well with My Soul," to name a few. Listen to them throughout the day or even as you settle down to sleep.

When you are filled with tension, anxiety, and exhaustion, words of praise to the Lord can revive your heart and de-stress your body. Rest now in joyful singing. May your singing provide profound peace, rest, and alignment with God as you meditate and abide in Christ.

Dear heavenly Father, I thank you that you have given me a longing to meditate before you, to pray, and to study and pursue your Word. Help me sing like no one but you is listening. You are the only One who matters. So let me sing of your love, sing of your strength, sing of your presence and protection. In the name of Jesus, your Son, our Savior, and my Lord, amen.

MY SOUL FINDS REST: PSALM 62

Yes, my soul, find rest in God;
  my hope comes from him.
Truly he is my rock and my
  salvation;
  he is my fortress, I will not be
  shaken.

—PSALM 62:5-6

 While we often think of rest in terms of the physical, it also applies to the emotional and spiritual. How are you doing with rest for your soul?

I invite you to pour out your concerns to God and let your soul find perfect rest in his presence. Release all your strivings and pursuits of earthly gain to him. He alone is your rock, your salvation, your fortress.

You are safe with him. You are sheltered in his presence. In the midst of every trouble, he is with you. You are secure in his salvation, and he has built a wall of peace around you to protect and guard you.

We often think of castles and fortresses as things that protect our bodies. In medieval Europe, in the days of feudal kings when attacks were frequent, the people would all gather in the courtyard of the local castle to be safe from their enemies.

Picture God as that fortress for your soul. Are you assaulted on every side by Satan and the lies he tells you? Maybe you're dealing with serious health issues or job loss or a rebellious child. So many things can assail you from every side.

Instead of panicking, run into the shelter that is your God. He is impenetrable. He hands you the sword of the Spirit, which is the Word of God. He fastens the helmet of salvation on your head. He cannot be moved, and so you are safe. All your burdens are lifted onto his shoulders. All your concerns are in his hands. The enemy keeps coming against you, but you cannot be moved because you rest in God. You *can* rest.

What is wearying your soul? Feel the shelter of God's presence surround you like a tall fortress that cannot be broken. He is with you, comforting you. He is watching over you, and in him your soul finds rest.

Feel the calm presence of the Holy Spirit. Be reminded of his gentleness, his compassion, his grace. He is sheltering you with a fortress of safety and protection. You can fully depend on him. You don't need to trust in your own abilities, because God is able. You don't need to trust in riches, because God is your treasure. He is your confidence, and he will not disappoint.

Hear only the quiet voice of God's love as he surrounds you with his presence. Wait silently before God and put your hope in him. Your very life is in his hands. His Word rests deep in your mind. In him your soul finds rest.

Lord, I pray that in you alone I will find hope, rest, and peace. Help me to wait for you in silence, in peaceful expectation. Help me to release every concern to you and find your perfect rest. Help me trust in your guidance, in your holiness, and in your sovereignty. I ask for safety as I breathe deeply of your presence and your protection over me. Thank you for securing me in your salvation and for building a fortress of love around me, surrounding me with your peace. In the holy name of Jesus I pray. Amen.

NEVER FORGOTTEN: PSALM 105

For he remembered his holy
  promise
given to his servant Abraham.
He brought out his people with
  rejoicing,
  his chosen ones with shouts of
  joy.

—PSALM 105:42-43

 Do you ever feel forgotten? Today I invite you to center your heart on this truth: God always remembers you. Breathe it in deeply. As you slow down, tell your distracting thoughts to come back later, and focus in: God always remembers you.

In Psalm 105 the psalmist listed many ways God has

cared for his chosen people. God made a promise to Abraham, the psalmist reminded, and then, generations later, when Abraham's descendants were slaves in Egypt, God remembered his promise.

When you feel forgotten, you may feel like you're invisible to the people around you, like you don't matter. But God invites you to know the truth: you are valuable and beloved— and never forgotten. Let that truth move through your body, bringing joy, releasing tension, and lightening your spirit.

You may feel forgotten, but God has not forgotten you— and never will.

What a glorious promise! God will never leave you or forsake you. God will never forget you.

God remembers you. Let this truth fill your heart with joy today. Let it make your spirit light and buoyant.

God loves you, but God doesn't want you to stay the same. God can deliver you from the sins that so easily entangle. Because of the Lord's great love, we are not consumed. God's mercies are new every morning. Every morning God remembers you with love and mercy.

The reason that God delivered his people from slavery in Egypt was that he had made a promise to Abraham. When God delivered his people, they responded with songs and joyful shouts. How do you respond when God delivers you?

Put yourself in the sandals of a child born into slavery in Egypt. Your people are oppressed, overworked, underfed, and exhausted. And then the pharaoh declares that all newborn babies must die.

Your parents gather the family together, and your mother whispers stories that have been passed down. "God promised our forefather Abraham that we would be fruitful and that we would have our own land one day," she says.

Strange things start happening in Egypt. A man named Moses appears and claims to speak for God. He says he's going to lead you to freedom. Could this be God's way of fulfilling his promise?

As you leave Egypt, you confess how much you'd doubted. You hadn't believed that after all these years God would still remember the promise, but you feel a song of joy welling up. God never forgets his promises.

The psalmist reminded God's people of all the ways God had been faithful in their history. As God has been faithful to remember you, be faithful to remember God.

Heavenly Father, thank you for choosing me to be your child and for giving me the Holy Spirit to be with me forever. I know that you always keep your promises, and that you will never forget me. Sometimes I do feel lost and forgotten; when that happens, help me to hold fast to you and to the truth that you tell me about who I am and how I fit in your family. Thank you for loving me. Amen.

GOD IS NEAR: PSALM 68

Praise be to the Lord, to God our
Savior,
who daily bears our burdens.

—PSALM 68:19

Does God ever seem distant to you?

Take a moment and let your mind drift to something far away, such as an item on the other side of the room. Imagine something on the other side of the house. A long-distance trip you've taken. The distance to the moon. A planet. A star. The very edge of the known universe. You and I are often reminded of how big and mighty and holy God is, and that is absolutely true. God is pure holiness and lives outside of time. He created the tallest mountains and carved the deepest oceans. His laws are high and holy.

However, because of Jesus Christ we can draw near to God and he comes near to us. Jesus has removed our sin so that you and I can have a relationship with God. Not only that, but he also loves us intimately, fills us with his Spirit, and surrounds us with love. We are his and he is ours. The veil is torn so that we may now be in God's presence, full of joy and abounding in love. Like a good parent, he is near to us. He helps us and protects us, and when we fall and are hurting, he carries us in his arms, close to his heart.

Our Jesus is Savior. He is Redeemer. He is the king of the universe, now and forever. And he cares for you. Today, if you are feeling alone or far away from God, remember that he loves you. He always hears you when you speak with him. He picks you up when you stumble. He provides for you daily, and he is always close to you. He will never leave you or abandon you.

Allow that truth to really sink in for a moment.

He carries you in his arms; he bears your burdens. The images are slightly different but point to the same idea: he is a God who takes the hard things, the heavy things, right out of our arms. When we struggle to press forward in this journey of a life, he doesn't encourage from afar—he actively enters into our lives and uses his power to help us.

Our God is a helper. Helping is not a subservient role; a helper is a support beam, the one who bears the weight and the stress to keep the structure standing.

Imagine your weak point. Now imagine the power and strength of the God who built the mountains and set the planets into orbit. Imagine that strength running straight through your weak point like a support beam.

The word the psalmist uses to describe a God who helps? *Savior.* He doesn't simply lay down tools and instruct us how to help ourselves. No. He is *the* Savior of our lives, our souls, our eternity. He saves us, and he makes us new.

Oh God who hears me even now, I am yours and you are mine! Thank you for loving me with an everlasting love. Help me to praise and thank you for being my king and ruler, my rescuer from sin and death, and my Father who loves me. Thank you that your Word tells us that you are love, and that you surround us with joyous singing. When I am afraid, feel all alone, or just removed from you, would you remind me of the truth of your nearness? Would you please let me feel your presence? Remind me that I am your child and that you hear me and love me, even when I don't feel like it. Thank you that you tend to me like a shepherd and carry me close to your heart. Thank you for knowing me by name. Thank you for engraving my name on your hands. It's impossible for you to forget me! I love you. Amen.

SAFE HARBOR: PSALM 107

They were glad when it grew calm,
and he guided them to their
desired haven.

—PSALM 107:30

 Life sometimes takes us into choppy waters. Hanging on for dear life, we find ourselves off course, in need of a safe harbor—a place where we can feel comfortable, peaceful, and anchored in God's protection. That may be where you are right now, in need of rest and a word from the Lord.

If so, I invite you to picture a busy port. As you look around, you see boats headed in different directions. Some are headed out to sea, while others are headed for port.

Others seem to be merely drifting, going one way and then another, oblivious to the changing conditions.

Storm clouds begin to roll in, blocking the bright sun. They silently loom over your crew. In anticipation you scramble across the teetering deck to your assigned position.

Shadows swallow the last rays of light, and thunder rumbles through the air. Rain begins to pour furiously, drowning any sight of certainty. Monstrous waves of contrasting shades slam your boat.

The waves break around the rocks in the shallows, their foamy crests chaotically swirling downward, disconcerting you, the movement of the water muddying your thoughts as you call upon the Lord.

Eventually things calm down and you're thankful you've crossed the rough waters. The waves have subsided, yet the air is still damp and foggy. Through the fog, a glimmer of light shines dimly. The golden beam slowly rotates. It's a lighthouse, shining the way for weary captains and their crews to enter a safe harbor. This beacon of hope has stood strong and weathered the storm.

While your cargo has bounced around and you are a little rattled, you've survived the worst of the storm; you are in one piece. You slowly steer your boat further into the harbor, where you can see more clearly. Nestled in a small inlet is a mooring perfect for your long-anticipated respite.

You know that if boats are not secured, they can drift away if a storm occurs at night, so you make sure your lines are tight. Once you and your fellow travelers are securely anchored, you feel the gentle rocking of your vessel from side to side as tiny waves softly lap against the side of your boat. Your soul finds comfort. God's hand protects you. He has delivered you through the storm.

God is your safe harbor of consistent hope and endless love. Invite him into the deepest parts of you, and he will anchor you to a place where all things work together for the good for those who love him.

When the storms rage and the winds blow, when the waves are high, when our hearts are shaken and strength and courage seem to melt away, remember the One and Only, the One whom the wind and waves obey, the Lord Most High who can calm any storm.

He speaks, "Peace! Be still!"

Father, help me to continue my journey in trust, knowing that you will never fail me and that your divine purpose in my life cannot be stopped by the enemy. I pray that you will give me a very real sense of your presence in all that is going on in my life. Equip my body, my vessel, for the days and weeks ahead. I pray that you will fill my sails with your peace and open my eyes to know that you are with me despite the fierce storm that is all around me. Help me to look to you and only you for strength and shelter. Help me to know that my hope and my safe harbor are found in you and your protection. Thank you for always being present with me and for loving me unconditionally and completely. Knowing that, I can confidently rest in a relationship with you. Oh Lord, hear the cries of my heart. I pray these things in the name of Jesus. Amen and amen.

NO FEAR IN FALLING:
PSALM 94

When I said, "My foot is slipping,"
　　your unfailing love, LORD,
　　　　supported me.
When anxiety was great within me,
　　your consolation brought me joy.

−PSALM 94:18−19

You've probably seen the old television commercial with the poor woman lying on the ground, crying out, "I've fallen, and I can't get up!" We may laugh at the commercial, but how often have you felt like you've fallen, or even been pushed down, and you don't know how you're going to get up and keep going?

Maybe you still feel like you're on the floor—like you're unable to get up from the fear, depression, or shame that you've fallen into. However, know that God's unfailing love is always supporting you, even when you are on the floor. When doubts fill our minds, God's comfort gives us renewed hope and cheer. Let God speak peace to your heart.

Like a child who falls while learning to walk, we can be assured that our gracious heavenly Father is there to pick us up. You wouldn't berate your child for falling, and your heavenly Father does not condemn you.

The heavy weight of the burdens we carry in our hearts quite often makes us slip and fall. We become off balance. What are you carrying in your heart that is making you walk off balance? Do anxious thoughts multiplying within you make you feel unstable? Do they make your feet slip and fall? Imagine in that moment that God is holding you up. He's catching you. What a strong, safe feeling that is!

Consider your response after God catches you. Is it to leave and return to your own strength? Or is it to linger in the tender, loving, compassionate arms you were always meant to be in? Picture it. Imagine your response. Your heavenly Father comes with his love. He keeps you steady. He comforts you. He makes you feel secure with a steady, comforting love.

After he helps you up, resist the desire to dust yourself off and look around to see if anyone noticed. Instead, imagine yourself turning back to him. Walk into the tender, loving, compassionate arms of Christ in all your dishevelment.

You don't have to be afraid of falling. That can hinder

you from stepping out in faith. But remember that when you do fall, God is there to help you.

Dear God of promises and protection, remind me of your compassion and loving-kindness. Remind me that you will hold me up. Even when my anxious thoughts multiply within me, remind me that your comforts will delight me. You see falls before I do. You think faster than I do. You move faster than I do. You are stronger than I am. Hold me, dear Father. Hold me when I fall. In the name of Jesus I offer and acknowledge this in prayer. Amen.

HOLY REST: PSALM 138

I will praise you, Lord, with all my
    heart;
      before the "gods" I will sing your
        praise.
I will bow down toward your holy
    temple
    and will praise your name
      for your unfailing love and your
        faithfulness,
for you have so exalted your
    solemn decree
    that it surpasses your fame.
When I called, you answered me;
    you greatly emboldened me.

—PSALM 138:1–3

In Psalm 138 the psalmist expressed his love for the Lord because God hears and answers his children when they call to him. Throughout the Psalms, he recalled the many troubles and sorrows he had already encountered, and how gracious and compassionate God had been to him—the Lord heard his cry for help and rescued him. He felt his soul strengthened by God's words and promises.

He could find holy rest.

Imagine yourself outdoors near the close of a warm and pleasant day. You are standing near a pond that is calm and clear, the surface smooth. As the evening hours draw nigh, the night sky provides a covering for your holy rest. Crickets begin to chirp, alerting you that it's time for sleep.

You follow a pathway that takes you to a perfect place, a place to sit all by yourself under a tall tree. A feeling of calm comfort and rest settles over you.

You know others have been here before you, for you spot a fire circle near where you're sitting. The smooth stones look like sentinels surrounding ash from previous fires. Stacks of kindling and wood stand nearby. You build a small fire. Within just a few minutes the dry kindling glows brightly, igniting the larger pieces of wood.

The tall tree and its piney aroma make the perfect spot to find holy rest.

Your tensions begin to melt away, along with the busyness of city life. You hear sounds all around you: bullfrogs, night birds calling, the crackling of the fire stirred by a gentle, cooling breeze.

Eventually, among the bird calls, you hear a soothing voice singing a delightful song. It seems to be coming from the trees. You hold very still as you listen, the words floating to you on the breeze.

"I have loved you with an everlasting love," the voice sings. "I have drawn you with unfailing kindness" (Jeremiah 31:3).

Your heart sings with this sweet voice as it continues, "The LORD is good to all; he has compassion on all he has made" (Psalm 145:9).

As your eyes scan the woods for the bearer of that voice, you see a figure dressed in white emerge from the woods. You have no fear, because the words of his song have filled your heart with joy and peace.

As the figure walks toward you, the singing continues: "For the LORD is good and his love endures forever; his faithfulness continues through all generations" (Psalm 100:5).

Finally, he is close enough for you to recognize. It's Jesus! He comes closer, still singing of his love for you as he takes a seat beside you next to the fire. Your heart bursts with joy. Your Savior and Lord is here by your side.

You sing in response, "Sovereign LORD, you are God! Your covenant is trustworthy, and you have promised these good things to your servant" (2 Samuel 7:28).

The sweet interchange between you continues with his words and your response as you sit side by side in perfect peace. He says, "Taste and see that the LORD is good; blessed is the one who takes refuge in him" (Psalm 34:8).

You respond, "The LORD is good, a refuge in times of trouble. He cares for those who trust in him" (Nahum 1:7).

Jesus smiles into your eyes. Your beloved brother. Your Savior. Your friend. Your heart exults in God your Savior.

What blessed peace God brings with his very presence in your life. You can talk to him all day long, and he will bring rest to your soul.

Thank you, Father, for the innumerable ways you demonstrate your love, protection, and provision. Thank you for your love, compassion, and grace. I praise you because you are in control of all things. Give me greater faith to submit to your will in every facet of my life. Give me peace in the time of storms and rest when I am weary. Use me to help others as they seek to live for you. Help me let loose of my own desires so that your will can be my own. I thank you and praise you in the name of Jesus. Amen.

THE ETERNAL GOD: PSALM 90

Lord, you have been our dwelling
place
throughout all generations.
Before the mountains were born
or you brought forth the whole
world,
from everlasting to everlasting
you are God.

—PSALM 90:1-2

Imagine you are living during the time of Moses, long before the life of Christ.

You and the Israelites are camped on the east side of the Jordan River. You've had a long day of work. Your muscles are tired. Your bones are too. You want to rest, so you sit down in the green grass and enjoy the cool breeze off the river. It's refreshing on your skin. You take in the scents too—the smell of moisture in the air. The aroma of wildflowers. The fragrance of trees blooming.

Suddenly your ears attune to a conversation between Moses and some children. One of the children asks a question that piques your interest: "Who made God?"

"No one made God," Moses answers. "God has always existed. Throughout all generations, God has been our home. Before the mountains were born, he gave birth to the earth and the world. From beginning to end, he is God. We are merely dust. We are mortal. But God is spirit. He always has been. He is the everlasting God. To him, a thousand years is like a day."

As Moses finishes talking to the children, you look up at the sky. It's darker now, and the heavens are filling with stars. There are too many to count. You gaze at the Big Dipper. You find the constellation Orion. You locate the Pleiades. Suddenly a meteor—a shooting star—races through the sky. You are drawn to prayer—and worship.

Take a few moments now to reflect on what it means that God is eternal. Before the mountains were born, God was there. Before the earth and the world were created, he loved you. From beginning to end, he is God. To him, a thousand years is like a day.

God has always existed. Everything around you had a beginning, but not God. He had no beginning.

God is not constrained by time. He's not constrained by

space. God is the Alpha and the Omega. He is the everlasting God.

Before the universe was made, God had a plan for your life. He doesn't make it up as you go along. He's always been there for you. He's your home. He will never leave you. You will live with him forever.

Dear Father, you are the infinite God, the God who never sleeps. You are the eternal God. I am in awe of you. Before time began, you had a plan for my life. You always watch over me and protect me. You are the Alpha and the Omega, the Beginning and the End. You understand my life more than I do. May I find comfort in this truth. Grant me patience, peace, and refreshment so that I can serve you and others. In Christ's name I pray. Amen.

AT REST IN HIS STRONG ARMS: PSALM 91

Whoever dwells in the shelter of the
Most High
will rest in the shadow of the
Almighty.
I will say of the Lᴏʀᴅ, "He is my
refuge and my fortress,
my God, in whom I trust."

—PSALM 91:1-2

 Moses had just finished the work of building the tabernacle in the desert. How glorious he had found his God! How clearly he had felt God's presence and protection. God's people had not perished in their wandering. They had not been overcome by their enemies. They had been led by the pillar of fire by night and the pillar of cloud by day. They had been kept by God, and Moses rejoiced. He knew where his help had come from. It had come from the Lord, the maker of heaven and earth.

Psalm 91 speaks of abiding with God, sheltering in his presence. Imagine being in a castle tall and strong, built on a hill. No enemy can reach you. No harm can come to you. Arrows fly toward you, but the ramparts deflect them.

> Whoever dwells in the shelter of the Most High
> will rest in the shadow of the Almighty.
> I will say of the LORD, "He is my refuge and my fortress,
> my God, in whom I trust."

God is our strong fortress. We abide in him. We take up our shield of faith in our God whom we trust. No fiery arrows will find us. We are safe. We are in his strong arms.

As you walk along the path of life, sometimes the way is dark. Hunters seek you; traps surround you. But God has promised that you will not be captured. Nothing can snatch you out of his hands. Though evil surrounds you, you will not fall prey to it. God is your deliverer.

Night and day, you abide in God's presence. He provides and protects. You can be at perfect peace because these are God's promises to you. The terror of the night is not to be feared. The arrows of the day cannot touch you. All the evil that seeks to devour you will be turned away. You will not be destroyed. God is always by your side.

You belong to the Lord Jesus. You have been sealed by

the Holy Spirit of God. A branch in the vine, you abide in Jesus, and he in you (John 15:5). All that you do is appointed by him and protected by him. You have made the choice to live in his presence. To dwell not just *with* him, but *in* him.

Take a moment to imagine that you are surrounded by shining angels who have been given the job of protecting you. Of being by your side. Of keeping you from harm. Because you are God's precious child. The evil one knows this. He used these words from Psalm 91:11–12 to try to tempt Jesus in the desert:

> For he will command his angels concerning you
>> to guard you in all your ways;
> they will lift you up in their hands,
>> so that you will not strike your foot against a stone.

You have the authority in the name of Jesus to fight every attack of the enemy. To take every thought captive. Let the peace of Christ fill you as you rest in the assurance that God is watching over you. He protects you because he loves you and you are his beloved child.

Father God, as you have promised to do, watch over me as I go about my day and as I sleep tonight. Wash away all my fear in the fountain of your peace. Remember your promises, Oh Lord, that you would bless me and keep me; that you would make your face to shine upon me and be gracious to me; that you would lift up your countenance upon me and give me peace. I love you, Lord. I abide in your shadow. I find rest beneath your wings. I find glory in your presence. In the name of Jesus, amen.

SEEN BY GOD: PSALM 11

The Lord is in his holy temple;
the Lord is on his heavenly
throne.
He observes everyone on earth;
his eyes examine them.

—PSALM 11:4

 As God looks upon the earth, we know that nothing is beyond his loving gaze. He sees it all. He knows our thoughts, our habits, and our ways of doing things. He is faithful and just to forgive us when we confess our sins and failures to him. But most of all, he loves us through it all. He can be trusted with every single thing in our lives. He is able to handle it. We simply need to surrender all of our ways to him. He's got this. He sees you.

Nothing is better than a safe and secure place to rest in the comfort of your creator.

Trust that God never takes his eyes off of you. Envision the Lord in his holy temple. See him sitting on his throne, high and lifted up. Feel comforted that he is all-knowing, all-seeing, and all-powerful. He observes your life through the lens of his Son—the lens of love and mercy. And though he sits on his throne as sovereign Lord, his Spirit is ever indwelling you and surrounding you. You are never out of his reach or his sight. Rest in God's ever-attentive love and mercy.

Proverbs 15:3 says, "The eyes of the Lord are everywhere, keeping watch on the wicked and the good."

Behold the Lord
Faithful and true.
Behold your King
Who works righteousness in you.

Behold his eyes
Watching in love.
Through the lens of grace
And his Son above.

God looks to and fro, throughout the earth. His tireless gaze seeks goodness among his children. He watches so that he can strengthen you. We know this to be true because 2 Chronicles 16:9 says, "For the eyes of the Lord range throughout the earth to strengthen those whose hearts are fully committed to him." Sometimes you may feel unseen.

You may cry out, "God, can you see me?" The resounding answer to that question is "Yes!" He sees you. He is El Roi, or "the God who sees me," as Hagar called him in the wilderness (Genesis 16:13–14).

And because he sees you, he wants to be seen *by* you. Oswald Chambers wrote, "We will see God reaching out to us in every wind that blows, every sunrise and sunset, every cloud in the sky, every flower that blooms, and every leaf that fades, if we will only begin to use our blinded thinking to visualize it."[9]

Visualize the hand of God reaching through the heavens, breaking through the noise to comfort. Hear the calmness of his voice, speaking words of life over you. Picture sunsets over hills of glory, dotted with flowers that fill the landscape. See the clouds drift away as the holy presence of God parts them. His eyes are everywhere, keeping watch. He is strong on behalf of those whose hearts are loyal.

Heavenly Father, cover me with the countenance of your love. Wrap me in your arms of safety, and stay with me always. With each breath I take, fill me with the fullness of your peace. And with each breath I release, let it be as a sweet surrender to you. For you are with me. Your holiness surrounds me. Your eyes behold me. Thank you, kind and loving Father, for your precious promises. Thank you for your watchful gaze of serenity and peace. In the holy name of Jesus I pray these things. Amen.

THE GATES OF THE LORD: PSALM 100

Enter his gates with thanksgiving
and his courts with praise;
give thanks to him and praise
his name.

—PSALM 100:4

 Imagine yourself worshiping with God's people in Jerusalem in ancient Israel. The walk to the temple usually takes about ten minutes, but today you're taking your time, enjoying God's scenic creation.

Overhead a small puffy cloud drifts gently across a bright blue sky, like a tiny sailboat crossing the Mediterranean Sea. Just below the cloud, an eagle—unmistakable with its wide wingspan and snowy white tail—is enjoying the day, gliding through the breeze while hunting its next meal. It dominates the sky, and no other bird dares enter its territory.

The eagle reminds you of a story from the Pentateuch—how God rescued your people from the Egyptians, symbolically carrying you on eagles' wings and bringing you to himself.

Near the end of your path, you pass an olive tree and enjoy the sights and sounds of a Sinai rosefinch—a bird as colorful as its name. Its head and chest boast multiple shades of red—as if God himself painted it with a thousand roses from the garden of Eden before teaching it to fly. The cheerful rosefinch chirps as you slowly pass by. You're hoping it doesn't fly away. Thankfully, it doesn't notice you, and it stays perched on a small branch, singing beautifully as if it knows it's time to worship.

A few minutes later, you arrive outside the temple—the temple built by Solomon. It's the home of the ark of the covenant and the Ten Commandments given by God to Moses on Mount Sinai. That thought alone gives you chills as you anticipate God's presence.

The temple itself is magnificent: made of cedar and stone, it is the largest building around—a glorious structure for a worthy God.

Finally, you enter the temple gates. Several hundred people have already gathered to worship in the courtyard. They are smiling and laughing.

Suddenly the sound of trumpets fills the air, followed by

drums and cymbals. You've heard this melody and rhythm before, but it always sparks emotions in you—even tears of joy. It's the sound of God's people worshiping.

You can feel God's presence in the temple. He has blessed your people and has blessed you too—with food, with friends and family, with peace, with safety. He revealed himself with signs and wonders, rescued his people from Egypt, and has promised to take care of you forever.

Most of all, he has blessed you by giving you hope for eternity.

Do you ever wish you were as blessed as the people of Israel were? Did you know you already are? They looked forward to the coming Messiah. But you know Christ. You are living in the days they longed to see! Blessed be the name of the Lord.

Dear Holy God, I long to be in your presence. Help me to know that I can worship you in spirit and in truth because you are Spirit and you are truth. You are worthy of all of my praise. In your presence is fullness of joy. My body is now your temple. That is an awesome truth. Thank you for living in me. In the name of Jesus I pray. Amen.

BROKEN AND
BEAUTIFUL: PSALM 103

For as high as the heavens are
above the earth,
so great is his love for those who
fear him;
as far as the east is from the west,
so far has he removed our
transgressions from us.

—PSALM 103:11-12

 You may feel that something inside you is broken because of your sin, and that God can't look at you because of it. But God sees you as beautiful because Jesus cleansed you from your sin.

"As high as the heavens are above the earth." That's how deep God's love is for us. "As far as the east is from the west."

Knowing your sin will never again be brought up by your heavenly Father should bring ecstatic joy to your heart.

Consider these words from Psalm 103. The distance from the heavens to the earth's surface, the span of land between the east and the west, is vast. In the time of ancient Israel, these distances would have been incomprehensible. These word pictures give us just a glimpse into how completely our sins are removed by the blood of Jesus. Let the truth of that sink deep into your soul today.

And then focus on another thought: your beauty is built from your brokenness.

Sometimes, even knowing that truth, you may wonder, *How can something that is broken ever be made beautiful again?* It may seem impossible, but in the Master Potter's hands, shards of clay can become a lovely vessel useful for God's work.

Transformation from broken to beautiful happens not because of our own effort but because of Christ's work of redemption on the cross. He understands what it's like to be human because he became human for our sakes.

Imagine taking a precious vase and using it as a hammer. That's not what it's meant for, and it will shatter that beautiful creation. Sometimes, despite our efforts to protect that vase, it can be shattered by someone else's selfish actions. Now imagine God, who created that vase in the first place, gently picking up the shattered pieces. There is no condemnation in his eyes, only sadness for the brokenness. You think maybe he is going to throw away those broken pieces because they are not useful to him anymore.

But then, to your surprise, he lovingly handles each broken piece—sorting, cleaning, straightening. You see tears in his eyes for the brokenness, but so much love that it squeezes your heart and you weep. As he touches each piece, it is transformed into something astonishingly beautiful.

Even though you can't quite see the whole design yet, know that God has taken each and every broken part of your story, your priceless vase, and is creating something even more valuable because it has been restored by his hands.

Father God, King David wrote the words of Psalm 103 by the power of your Holy Spirit. He knew of God's forgiveness. He had sinned deeply, but he had been called a man after God's own heart. I want to be a person after your heart. Help me to see myself as you see me—clean, holy, and beautiful. I know that you bring beauty from ashes. Like the mythical phoenix, I want to be brought back to life by your love, resurrected from my old life. Help me to die to myself and the sins of my past that hold me in bondage. Release me from my sin by the power of Jesus' blood. Wash me, and I will be whiter than snow. Amen and amen.

HIS GLORY, OUR GOOD: PSALM 8

Lord, our Lord,
   how majestic is your name in all
      the earth!

You have set your glory
   in the heavens.
Through the praise of children and
      infants
   you have established a
      stronghold against your
      enemies,
   to silence the foe and the
      avenger.

—PSALM 8:1–2

If anything is troubling you, anything at all, I encourage you to release it to God. Dear friend, offer your worries to him with open hands. He can handle them. Go ahead. Release all of your concerns to the Lord who loves you.

Today our Scripture focus is on the glorious words of praise from Psalm 8. This psalm of David might best be described as a song of God's glory, his majesty, displayed throughout the heavens.

> Lord, our Lord,
> > how majestic is your name in all the earth!
>
> You have set your glory
> > in the heavens.
> Through the praise of children and infants
> > you have established a stronghold against your
> > > enemies,
> > to silence the foe and the avenger.
> When I consider your heavens,
> > the work of your fingers,
> the moon and the stars,
> > which you have set in place,
> what is mankind that you are mindful of them,
> > human beings that you care for them?

"What is mankind that you are mindful of them?"
How is it possible that the creator of the universe has

time to be mindful of us? Surely he has better things to think about. And yet God's thoughts over us are of love and acceptance. After all, not only did his hands set the moon and stars in place; his hands fashioned each of us in his own likeness. Dear one, the Lord is mindful of you. He knows you. He thinks about you. He loves you. Let those thoughts bring you comfort and peace.

"What [are] . . . human beings that you care for them?"

Oh, how God cares for you! He cares about the smallest of details regarding your life. Feel his nurturing presence watching over you. You are his beloved child, and he holds you in his loving hands. There is no doubt that God is with you. For the Scriptures declare that he is "Immanuel," which means, "God with us."

Feel the presence of God, Immanuel, with you at this very moment.

The Lord has set his glory above the heavens. He has set the moon and stars in their places.

One nineteenth-century astronomer wrote, "What have we to tell of all the different varieties of stars? What of those most supremely glorious objects? What of the Milky Way? Such are a few of the questions which occur, when we ponder on the mysteries of the heavens."[10]

The mysteries of the heavens are no mystery to their creator, for he has set his glory *above* the heavens. Rest under the heavens that God has put into place as a vast covering of starlit wonder and glory.

On each of the historical flights of the space shuttle

Discovery, the crew was awakened each morning by song. These wakeup calls were a tradition of the NASA program, and the songs were selected by mission control.

One Sunday morning during orbit, John Glenn and the rest of the crew woke up to a song written by Chris Rice called "Hallelujahs," a song that speaks of the "cratered moon and sparrow's wings, O thunder's boom and Saturn's rings."[11] As they hovered far above the earth with a miraculous view of God's handiwork, the astronauts were filled with a song of worship to the maker of the universe.

Let your soul resound with hallelujahs for the creator of all things.

Heavenly Father, I praise you for settling everything into its place so perfectly. Underneath the blanket of the starry heavens, you have assigned us our proper place. I pray for rest and peace in your presence. I ask that your glory will continue to shine in my life for my ultimate good. As the earth continues to spin on its axis and make its orbit around the sun, I pray my life will continue to flow under the mighty direction of your hand. Thank you that you are mindful of us, that you care about us, and that you love us. In the holy name of Jesus, amen.

A PRACTICE FOR EVERY DAY: PSALM 96

Worship the Lord in the splendor of
his holiness;
tremble before him, all the
earth.

—PSALM 96:9

 You were created to worship God. Did you know
that? That's what life is all about: praising the One
who is worthy of all our praise.

God is great, and greatly to be praised. With every breath,
praise the Lord! God calls you to worship him because it's
only in worshiping him that you come to understand who
you are and what you were made to do.

What does praising God feel like in your body? Think
about how your body responds when you speak words of

PEACE WITH THE PSALMS

gratitude or worship. Maybe your face softens into a smile. Maybe you lean forward a bit. Maybe you raise your hands.

In Psalm 96:9 the psalmist said to tremble before God. Think about the kinds of things that make you tremble. Fear, anxiety, excitement. Those are all things that can cause our bodies to react with a quivering of muscles. So how is trembling before God different? God is immense and powerful, but he doesn't want us to be afraid. We can tremble in awe. Let that thought sit for a moment.

Psalm 96 contains repeated commands to worship and praise the Lord. This isn't optional. And it's not something to do only when you feel like it. It's a practice that should be a part of your daily life. To praise God, you have to know God. What is something you know about God that makes your heart want to sing in praise to him?

Spend some time in the rest of Psalm 96.

> Sing to the LORD a new song;
>> sing to the LORD, all the earth.
> Sing to the LORD, praise his name;
>> proclaim his salvation day after day.
> Declare his glory among the nations,
>> his marvelous deeds among all peoples.
>
> For great is the LORD and most worthy of praise;
>> he is to be feared above all gods.
> For all the gods of the nations are idols,

but the LORD made the heavens.
Splendor and majesty are before him;
     strength and glory are in his sanctuary.

Ascribe to the LORD, all you families of nations,
     ascribe to the LORD glory and strength.
Ascribe to the LORD the glory due his name;
     bring an offering and come into his courts.
Worship the LORD in the splendor of his holiness;
     tremble before him, all the earth.
Say among the nations, "The LORD reigns."
          The world is firmly established, it cannot be
               moved;
          he will judge the peoples with equity.

Let the heavens rejoice, let the earth be glad;
     let the sea resound, and all that is in it.
Let the fields be jubilant, and everything in them;
     let all the trees of the forest sing for joy.
Let all creation rejoice before the LORD, for he comes,
     he comes to judge the earth.
He will judge the world in righteousness
     and the peoples in his faithfulness.

Isn't it sweet to reflect on the ways that God's love has changed your life? Let praise be the practice you return to every day, no matter what you face.

Glorious God, your greatness is beyond what I can even imagine. I praise you for your wisdom, your power, and your love. Thank you for bringing me into your kingdom through your Son, Jesus, and for sending your Spirit to be with me forever. Help me to live a life filled with praise and gratitude, even when things are difficult. I love you, Lord of all creation. I praise you for your mighty works. All the earth bows before you. You alone are worthy of our worship. Thank you for all that you've done for me in Christ. Make my life a living sacrifice of praise to you. In the name of Jesus I pray. Amen.

NOTHING IS UNKNOWN TO GOD: PSALM 139

You have searched me, LORD,
   and you know me.
You know when I sit and when I rise;
   you perceive my thoughts from afar.
You discern my going out and my
      lying down;
   you are familiar with all my ways.

—PSALM 139:1-3

 Have you experienced a period of time in your life that felt unknown and out of control? The truth is, we don't ever know what our future holds, but we serve a God who is sovereign: He is all-knowing and in control. We are reminded in Psalm 139 that nothing is unknown to God.

The reality is that control is an illusion. We may often feel powerful over our own lives, but in actuality we rest in God's hands. Thankfully, he is a God we can trust.

Did you catch how often the psalmist used the word *know* in Psalm 139:1–3? God knows when we sit and rise; he knows our thoughts and our words before we speak them. The psalmist even said, "You are familiar with all my ways."

Consider the ways you are known to God. What does this cause your heart to feel? As you think about the current unknowns in your life, what comfort do you find in God's sovereignty?

As the unknowns mount, as sometimes they do, what if you saw those times as an opportunity to know God more? Though there is so much that you cannot know, the God of the universe makes himself known to you through his Word and through his Spirit.

When you think about your current rhythms of life, what role does knowing God play? God knows us fully and invites us to know him in return. In fact, the joy of everlasting life is to know him.

The final verses of Psalm 139 say, "Search me, God, and know my heart; test me and know my anxious thoughts. See if there is any offensive way in me, and lead me in the way everlasting."

Let's look at those two verses phrase by phrase.

"Search me, God, and know my heart." The sovereignty of God means that he is all-knowing, yet the psalmist still implored God to know his heart. Imagine that you are the psalmist—though God already knows you, delight him by inviting him to know you.

"Test me and know my anxious thoughts." It is easy to find your thoughts becoming anxious when you feel out of control. What would happen if you exchanged those thoughts with thoughts about God's nearness?

"See if there is any offensive way in me." The New Living Translation renders the last verse like this: "Point out anything in me that offends you." To add more depth, the Hebrew word used in this text paints the picture of an idol: "Point out any idols in my life." Has your loss of control revealed any idols in your life?

"Lead me in the way everlasting." In John 17:3 Jesus said that everlasting life is not just what we meet after death. No, it is knowing God here. To walk on the path of everlasting life is to deliberately pursue knowing him more.

Search your heart for the things you are tempted to control, things that might get in the way of you hearing from God. Confess these to him and accept his complete forgiveness.

Acknowledge God's nearness, even amid the unknown. Take a deep breath and ask God to remind you of his sovereignty wherever you are today.

Oh, great God, I could make a very long list of all the things I do not know about what the coming days will hold. But longer still would be a list written of your unending grace, love, and care for my soul. I don't like feeling out of control. This unexpected season has caused me to realize that I might not have as much control as I thought I did. I find hope in the promise that you have not lost control. Help me to trust in your sovereignty as I wait for the future to unfold. While I battle anxious thoughts of the days to come, would you help me find rest in your sovereignty? You know what is to come, and that is enough for me. Amen.

HIS LOVE ENDURES FOREVER: PSALM 136

Give thanks to the Lord, for he is good.
His love endures forever.

—PSALM 136:1

God's steadfast love endures forever—from before
the beginning, from before there was time, and
extending into a future you can't yet see, into
eternity. God's steadfast love *is*. God's love is the steadfast
foundation of all that has been, all that is, and all that will be.

In Psalm 136 the psalmist praised God for a litany of
things he had done in the past to show his love. God made
the heavens and the earth, the sun, moon, and stars; God
delivered his people out of Egypt and led them through the
wilderness; God gave his people a home and protected them
against their enemies.

Let your worries and fears melt away in the face of the one thing that will outlast all of them: God's steadfast love.

The psalmist used two words to describe God's love, and each one is a weighty word that describes something that lasts: *enduring* and *forever*. If there was one thing the psalmist wanted to emphasize, it's that this love is not running out. How does your heart respond to the never-ending-ness of God's love?

The psalmist encouraged his readers to give thanks to the Lord in response to God's steadfast love. It's not always easy to give thanks. Sometimes God's love doesn't feel close at hand. But even when days are dark and it's hard to find joy, it is still good to give thanks to the Lord. Practice the discipline of giving thanks, whether or not you feel like it.

God's steadfast love stretches further back than you can remember and further forward than you can imagine. God's love for you was present at the moment time began, when he created the heavens and the earth. Put yourself there, in that first garden, and watch as God's love brings forth sky and sea, plants and animals.

God's steadfast love was present in your ancestors' lives. What do you know of their stories? Picture your grand-parents and great-grandparents, and the way God's steadfast love touched their lives. Whether they knew God or not, his love was present in the rain that fell and the sun that shone.

God's mercy carries you even today. Call to mind the things that fill your life: your family and friends, your work and your leisure time, your sickness and health. How do you see God's love in it all?

God's steadfast love extends into the future, a faithful and steadfast love that will see you through whatever comes. Hold your hopes and dreams before God now, and tell him that you trust him to be faithful through whatever comes.

Think about people in your neighborhood or community who are in need spiritually, relationally, physically, mentally, emotionally, or financially. People who are struggling and could use your support and encouragement. How can you concretely express this merciful attitude that is grounded in God's love? God's love and mercy are not gifts to keep for yourself. They are gifts to be shared with the whole world. Ask God to help you find one way today to share his love with someone.

Let your heart respond with gratitude to God for his never-failing love and mercy. They endure forever. Hold fast to that thought as you go about your day and even as you lie down to sleep. Let it permeate your dreams.

Faithful God, thank you for your loving-kindness—the one thing I can always rely on, the steadfast foundation that extends from before I can remember and through to the future I can't yet see. You are a faithful God. Help me to understand how great your steadfast love is for me. You know the thoughts and feelings I bring before you. You know my fears, my worries, my sadness, and my joys. I give them to you now. I am trusting your mercy and your steadfast love, and I believe they will carry me through everything. In the name of Jesus I pray. Amen.

GUARDING WHAT YOU SAY: PSALM 141

Set a guard over my mouth, LORD;
keep watch over the door of my
lips.

—PSALM 141:3

 The Crown Jewels of the United Kingdom are protected in the Jewel House—a section of the Tower of London—by bomb-proof glass, one hundred hidden cameras, and more than fifty trained military officials. These relics are extremely valuable and are treated as such.

Psalm 141:3 shows us how to guard something even more precious than these treasures: our words.

Your words hold greater value than any jewel, because they have the power to speak life or to speak evil. Like a spark in a dry forest, your words can ignite a blaze of emotion, or they can be cooling water to a hot situation. They have the power to help others accomplish the impossible and can influence someone to do the unthinkable, or they can hold someone back from stretching their wings. Because of your words' potential influence, guarding them is vital.

King David prayed that God would set a guard over his mouth. He understood the impulsive nature of his lips and therefore relied on God to help him.

Maybe you have told a "white lie" out of convenience or have gossiped to fit in with the crowd. If you want God to help you guard your words, you must give him access to every part of your heart. Jesus teaches that people speak the words that come from their heart (Luke 6:45). Only when we surrender our whole hearts to him will the words that come out of our mouths be controlled.

If you are having a language problem, it might be a symptom of a heart problem. For instance, if you are gossiping, maybe the heart problem is insecurity. If you are sarcastic, the heart problem may be anger.

Sometimes it seems that the tongue has a mind of its own. James 3:8 says that no human being can tame the tongue. That's why we need God to be the guardian over what we say. He can do what we cannot.

The amazing truth about this verse is that the Lord desires to help you guard what you say. We know that all things are possible with God, and so we know that our tongues can indeed be tamed if we set God as the guardian of our mouths.

Take a moment to rest, knowing that God loves you so much that he wants to protect your heart and your words. He knows we cannot tame our tongues ourselves, so he helps us in our weakness. Instead of wrestling with guilt, rest in the grace you have in Jesus Christ, and trust him for help in this area with which all of us struggle. Give it to him now.

Dear heavenly Father, I thank you for giving me this time to reflect upon you and the gift of this day you have given me. I pray that my words will reflect who you are in my life. Guard my lips from speaking ill of you or of others. I thank you for entrusting me with the power of my voice. Thank you for giving me a story to tell and relationships in which to share life. I pray that you will help me learn how to use my words for good and not harm. Help me become more like Jesus by studying his example. Guard my words as well as my heart. It's in the name of Jesus that I pray, amen.

EVERY KNEE SHALL BOW: PSALM 95

Come, let us bow down in worship,
let us kneel before the Lord our
Maker.

—PSALM 95:6

Psalm 95:6 creates a beautiful word picture.

There are so many reasons to kneel before Jesus. There is desperation, like the leper in Mark 1 who humbled himself before Jesus, asking to be healed. There is a love for others, like the mother in Mark 7 whose daughter was tormented by a demon.

But the knowledge of who God is, his character, should cause you to fall on your knees. He is your Lord, or to say it another way, he is your master. He has chosen you to be a sheep in his pasture, cared for so that you can be free of worry and stress, eating the lush fare he has provided.

God is also your maker. As the One who created you, he knows you because he formed you as his work of art. He knows your heart, desires, and longings. He also knows your weaknesses, your struggles. He, more than anyone else, knows what you are lacking and how he can meet your needs.

We have a penchant for praising someone who does awesome things. Like a sports figure who makes an amazing play or an actor or musician highly skilled in their craft. How much more awesome are the works of God? We are compelled to worship him for his mighty works.

Picture an artist creating a beautiful painting of a city. You are drawn to the vibrant colors, and then you see the shadows and darkness that you don't really like. God painted you with beauty and shadows. He wants to be with you, even in the shadows.

Or picture a potter, forming a vase on the potter's wheel as it spins around and around. Right now it's shapeless. As it rotates, the potter's hands, firm yet gentle, embrace the vase. He knows its purpose; he knows its possibilities. As he places pressure in one location, he allows it to be free in others, causing it to take a unique shape. He knows the color glaze he's going to put on the outside, but more than anything, he knows the love he has felt in forming the inside.

And then there is the oven, the kiln, where the vase is baked. The potter knows the perfect temperature that will bake the vase without breaking it. He knows how long the vase needs to bake to become strong. He makes things that are perfect in his eyes.

In the next verse of Psalm 95, the psalmist reminds us, "For he is our God and we are the people of his pasture, the flock under his care."

This is a gentle reminder of who you are: "the people of [God's] pasture." Your maker wants to care for you by providing pastures, places of refreshment and rest. He has provided the place you are in right now to give you rest as you put your trust in him.

> *Lord, thank you that "every knee will bow" to you*
> *(Isaiah 45:23). Thank you for the way you have met*
> *the needs of those in Scripture as they knelt before you,*
> *and I know you will meet my needs as I kneel before*
> *you in my heart. Bless me as one of the sheep in your*
> *pasture. I know you hold me in your hand. Renew my*
> *spirit, I pray. Amen.*

PRAISE FOR ALL SEASONS: PSALM 150

Praise the Lord.

Praise God in his sanctuary;
    praise him in his mighty
        heavens.
Praise him for his acts of power;
    praise him for his surpassing
        greatness.
Praise him with the sounding of the
    trumpet,
    praise him with the harp and
        lyre,
praise him with timbrel and dancing,
    praise him with the strings and
        pipe,

> praise him with the clash of cymbals,
> praise him with resounding
> cymbals.
>
> Let everything that has breath
> praise the LORD.
>
> Praise the LORD.

—PSALM 150

 Most people have a favorite season of the year. Many have favorite aspects of every season. What do you enjoy the most? Maybe sunshine, the beach, and vacations during the summer. Maybe the colors of leaves, fresh air, and a cool breeze during autumn. Maybe falling snow, the fireplace warming the room, and hot chocolate warming your body during winter.

But our lives include seasons in other ways—seasons of joy followed by seasons of sadness. Seasons of celebration near seasons of grief.

Because of that, we do not always feel emotions that inspire us to give praise to God. We know we should, but feelings often get in the way. Many people see praise and worship as insincere when they're not "feeling it." But our emotional status and our external circumstances should not control our praise. We can learn the honor of thanking God in the middle of any season—aware of our feelings but praising God anyway. To rejoice is a choice. That does not mean faking your faith and pretending to possess narrow happiness when you are hurting. It doesn't suggest insincere singing. What it means is to see beyond the *now*.

Consider the many languages over many centuries in which this song has been offered in praise to God. Think of the many instruments used in that psalm. Think of how the nation of Israel used that poetic hymn to rejoice and celebrate God's goodness. Maybe Jesus sang this hymn in the temple.

Maybe you've noticed a person who seemed reluctant to sing during a church service one Sunday morning. The surrounding people looked happy. Their smiles almost annoyed the silent person as he or she was still struggling with the grief of an unanswered prayer. But hearing a song that included Psalm 150:6, that person realized that giving thanks was a choice he or she could make. Maybe you've been that person.

Most people feel on occasion that they just can't praise, but choosing to rejoice can bring freedom. Take time to notice the beauty around you. Dwell on the wonder of God's love. Realize that he will never leave you or forsake you. Remember the apostle Paul in 1 Thessalonians 5:18 instructing his audience to give thanks in every situation. That exhortation came from a man who knew persecution, rejection, and desperation. He found ways to rejoice in prison, in famine, and in isolation. Joining Paul in rejoicing can bring nourishment to our souls.

Life in this fallen world includes many seasons. Sometimes those seasons include storms. And at other times the land feels dry and the heat feels impossible to endure. But no matter what, lifting praise to God will bring refreshment to your soul.

> *Heavenly Father, today I choose to rejoice—for your creation, your wisdom, your guidance, your love, your grace. Through my pain and questions, you have given me assurance. You have never abandoned me. I sing songs of joy and give thanks. I also choose to thank you in advance for how you will guide me and provide for me. God, help me to embrace the larger truth in my personal relationship with you, the Creator who made me in your image. Hold me with you in hope, reminding me that you will never leave me nor forsake me. With every breath, I praise you. Amen.*

NOTES

1. "Did You Know?" Anxiety and Depression Association of America, accessed February 18, 2021, https://adaa.org /about-adaa/press-room/facts-statistics.
2. Courtney E. Ackerman, "23 Amazing Health Benefits of Mindfulness for Body and Brain," Positive Psychology.com, October 13, 2020, https://positivepsychology.com/benefits -of-mindfulness/.
3. Thomas A. Tarrants III, "Biblical Meditation," *Knowing & Doing* (Winter 2019), C.S. Lewis Institute, https://www .cslewisinstitute.org/Biblical_Meditation.
4. Thomas Chisholm, "Great Is Thy Faithfulness," 1923. Public domain.
5. Scott Krippayne, "What Breaks Your Heart," Spring Hill Music Group, 2001.
6. Dictionary.com, s.v. "joy," accessed February 18, 2021, https://www.dictionary.com/browse/joy?s=t.
7. Sandra Felton, *The Messies Manual: A Complete Guide to Bringing Order and Beauty to Your Home* (Grand Rapids: Revell, 2005). See also messies.com.

8. Math-Geography Lesson Plan, American Heart Association, accessed March 19, 2021, https://www.heart.org/idc /groups/heart-public/@wcm/@fc/documents/downloadable /ucm_454347.pdf.

9. Oswald Chambers, "Is Your Ability to See God Blinded?" *My Utmost for His Highest*, accessed February 18, 2021, https://utmost.org/is-your-ability-to-see-god-blinded/.

10. Robert Stawell Ball, *The Story of the Heavens* (London: Cassell, 1890), 2.

11. Chris Rice, "Hallelujahs," Warner Chappell Music, 1997.

Welcome to Abide.

We'll meet you right where you are.

Find daily inspiration

Overcome life's challenges

Calm your mind with God's peace

Be well with us.

Abide is a Christian wellness app designed to help you stress less and sleep better through guided, Bible-based meditations, bedtime stories, breathing exercises, and more.

Download Abide today to start your wellness journey and access our library of over 2,000 pieces of content, with new meditations added daily.